Indigenous and Local Communities and Protected Areas

Towards Equity and Enhanced Conservation

Guidance on policy and practice for Co-managed
Protected Areas and Community Conserved Areas

IUCN – The World Conservation Union

Founded in 1948, The World Conservation Union brings together States, government agencies and a diverse range of non-governmental organizations in a unique world partnership: over 1000 members in all, spread across some 140 countries.

As a Union, IUCN seeks to influence, encourage and assist societies throughout the world to conserve the integrity and diversity of nature and to ensure that any use of natural resources is equitable and ecologically sustainable. A central secretariat coordinates the IUCN Programme and serves the Union membership, representing their views on the world stage and providing them with the strategies, services, scientific knowledge and technical support they need to achieve their goals. Through its six Commissions, IUCN draws together over 10,000 expert volunteers in project teams and action groups, focusing in particular on species and biodiversity conservation and the management of habitats and natural resources. The Union has helped many countries to prepare National Conservation Strategies, and demonstrates the application of its knowledge through the field projects it supervises. Operations are increasingly decentralized and are carried forward by an expanding network of regional and country offices, located principally in developing countries.

The World Conservation Union builds on the strengths of its members, networks and partners to enhance their capacity and to support global alliances to safeguard natural resources at local, regional and global levels.

Cardiff University

The Department of City and Regional Planning, Cardiff University is pleased to be a partner in the production of this important series of guidelines for protected area planning and management. The Department, through its Environmental Planning Research Unit, is actively involved in protected areas research; runs specialised courses on planning and environmental policy; and has a large Graduate School offering opportunities for persons interested in pursuing research for a PhD or as part of wider career development. If you are interested in learning more about the Department, its research capabilities and courses please write to us at the address given below.

Professor Terry Marsden BAHon., PhD, MRTPI
Head of Department
Department of City and Regional Planning
Cardiff University
Glamorgan Building
King Edward VIIth Avenue
Cardiff, CF10 3WA, Wales, UK
Tel: + 44 2920 874022
Fax: + 44 2920 874845

Indigenous and Local Communities and Protected Areas

Towards Equity and Enhanced Conservation

Guidance on policy and practice for Co-managed
Protected Areas and Community Conserved Areas

Grazia Borrini-Feyerabend, Ashish Kothari and Gonzalo Oviedo

with inputs from Marco Bassi, Peter Bille Larsen,
Maurizio Farhan Ferrari, Diane Pansky and Neema Pathak

Adrian Phillips, Series Editor

World Commission on Protected Areas (WCPA)

Best Practice Protected Area Guidelines Series No. 11

**IUCN – The World Conservation Union
2004**

Published by: IUCN, Gland, Switzerland and Cambridge, UK

Citation: Borrini-Feyerabend, G., Kothari, A. and Oviedo, G. (2004). *Indigenous and Local Communities and Protected Areas: Towards Equity and Enhanced Conservation.* IUCN, Gland, Switzerland and Cambridge, UK. xviii + 111pp.

ISBN: 2-8317-0675-0

Cover photos: Front: A meeting in Urok (Formosa, Bijagos archipelago, Guinea Bissau) to discuss management issues regarding the local community conserved area (which includes marine and terrestrial components). *(Courtesy Grazia Borrini-Feyerabend).* Back (top to bottom): In India innumerable forests are considered to be sacred by the neighboring communities and left undisturbed as both ecosystems and biodiversity habitats. *(Courtesy Grazia Borrini-Feyerabend)*; In recently created protected areas in the Caribbean, the involvement of traditional resource users and local communities in planning and managing tasks is widely accepted, both in law and practice. *(Courtesy Jim Barborak)*; Through pastoral practices, human communities have been shaping their living landscapes for thousands of years. Many such landscapes have outstanding aesthetic and biodiversity value and are now protected under co-management schemes. *(Courtesy Andy Wilson and North York Moors National Park Authority, the United Kingdom)*; The Regional Natural Park of the Dolomiti d'Ampezzo (surrounding the resort of Cortina – site of winter Olympic Games and highest real estate value in the Italian Alps) is managed by a community organization—the Regole d'Ampezzo – which retained its autonomy and rules for over 1,000 years of recorded history. *(Courtesy Stefano Lorenzi and Regole d'Ampezzo)*

Layout by: Bookcraft Ltd, Stroud, UK

Produced by: IUCN Publications Services Unit

Printed by: Thanet Press, Margate, Kent, UK

Available from: IUCN Publications Services Unit

219c Huntingdon Road, Cambridge CB3 0DL, United Kingdom
Tel: +44 1223 277894
Fax: +44 1223 277175
E-mail: info@books.iucn.org
www.iucn.org/bookstore
A catalogue of IUCN publications is also available

The text of this book is printed on 90gsm Fineblade Extra made from low-chlorine pulp.

Table of contents

Preface

As Chairs of two IUCN Commissions, it was an immense privilege to work together for one of the first great conservation events of the second millennium – the Vth IUCN World Parks Congress in Durban, South Africa, September 2003. The three thousand-strong crowd uplifted us and made evident the richness and variety of the new, much broader and diverse constituency that supports conservation today. Possibly even more inspiring, a new spirit could be detected among the many and such varied faces that composed that crowd. That spirit is relatively new in the conservation arena and we can only describe it as "mature", certainly an attitude whose time had come. We mean that people seemed to refrain – at least for the most part – from bickering and complaining about the faults of others and focused their energy instead towards understanding issues, identifying common goals and shaping joint efforts. The Durban Accord and Action Plan are the clearest manifestations of this collective spirit of collaboration. They are a powerful statement from people from different regions, origins, institutions and walks of life, a call to join in openness and mutual trust towards a world in which protected areas are the jewel in the crown of "a just world that values and conserves nature".

If the Durban spirit is to guide us at least for the current decade, documents and tools such as the one you have in your hands are essential. We need to translate lofty goals and aspirations into practical, everyday terms; we need to figure out what is important, what is a priority, what can be done, and how it can be done. Incidentally, this is exactly why this WCPA Guidelines series was born, and we are here proud to introduce the first jointly sponsored WCPA-CEESP issue. This issue is due to the generous work of TILCEPA – the CEESP-WCPA Theme on Indigenous and Local Communities, Equity and Protected Areas and, in particular, of their Co-chairs – Grazia Borrini-Feyerabend and Ashish Kothari – and of Gonzalo Oviedo, a long-time member who recently took on the post of Senior Social Policy Advisor in the IUCN Secretariat. These colleagues and their collaborators have gathered here some of the more poignant technical advice of the Durban Congress and lessons distilled from the field. The statements and options for action they propose are not yet IUCN policy – although some may soon become so at the third World Conservation Congress in Bangkok, November 2004. They are, however, inspired by the Durban results and are fully in line with the Programme of Work on Protected Areas of the Convention on Biological Diversity, approved at its 7th Conference of the Parties in Kuala Lumpur in February 2004.

For practitioners in search of an open and flexible guide to engaging indigenous peoples and local communities in protected area management, little can be richer and more encompassing than this volume. Government managers and civil society actors alike will find here clear concepts and concrete advice for policy at the national, landscape and site levels. Importantly, the book can also usher a more widespread recognition and much better protection of existing Community Conserved Areas – a marvellous world-wide conservation asset unfortunately in great jeopardy today.

It is with these objectives in mind that we are proud to introduce this volume and we thank its authors who generously volunteered their time in crafting it. We also take the occasion to acknowledge Adrian Phillips – a fabulous editor for the guidelines series who can certainly feel uplifted by passing on his task with this volume, a concrete and helpful statement towards more collaborative and equitable protected areas in the years ahead.

Kenton Miller, Chair

IUCN World Commission on
Protected Areas

M. Taghi Farvar, Chair

IUCN Commission on Environmental,
Economic and Social Policy

Acknowledgements

The material illustrated and discussed in these Guidelines draws from available literature and the field experience of the authors but it is mostly based on the results of nine regional reviews and several papers commissioned by the Theme on Indigenous and Local Communities, Equity and Protected Areas (TILCEPA) – a joint endeavour of the IUCN Commission on Environmental, Economic and Social Policy (CEESP) and the World Commission on Protected Areas (WCPA) – as part of the Ecosystems, Protected Areas and Peoples (EPP) project of the World Resources Institute (WRI) and WCPA. The original reviews and papers (see the detailed list below) can be consulted through the site: www.iucn.org/themes/ceesp/Wkg_grp/TILCEPA/community.htm.

The authors would like to thank **Diane Pansky** and **Peter Bille Larsen** who generously provided inputs during the phases of writing and reviewing this volume, as well as **David Hughes**, who prepared an early chapter on community relationship with private protected areas, now not included because of space constraints (we hope it will be the subject of a future publication). The insights and care of the Series Editor, **Adrian Phillips**, have been unfailingly thorough and supportive and are most warmly acknowledged.

The regional reviews and papers that provided the "backbone" of this publication were written by members of TILCEPA and of the IUCN/CEESP Collaborative Management Working Group (CMWG) and include:

- **a regional review of Community Conserved Areas and Co-managed Protected Areas in Spanish-speaking South America by Gonzalo Oviedo** – with contributions from Jorge Nahuel (Argentina), Victoria Maldonado (Chile), Fiona Worthington (Colombia), Emilce Mora Jaime (Colombia), Santiago Kingman (Ecuador), Jorge Rivas (Ecuador), Ruth Sylva (Ecuador), Jorge Esteban Oviedo (Ecuador), Bart De Dijn (Suriname) and Kathryn Monk (Guyana).

- **a regional review of Community Conserved Areas and Co-managed Protected Areas in South Asia by Neema Pathak** (India) – with contributions from Anwarul Islam (Bangladesh), S.U.K. Ekaratne (Sri Lanka), Altaf Hussain (Pakistan) and Ashish Kothari (India).

- **a regional review of Community Conserved Areas and Co-managed Protected Areas in South-East Asia by Maurizio Farhan Ferrari** (Malaysia) – with contributions from U Ohn (Burma), Amanda Bradley (Cambodia), Toby Carson (Cambodia), Zulkifli Lubis (Indonesia), Rukka (Indonesia), Johnnes Tulungen (Indonesia), Cristina Eghenter (Indonesia), Amalia Nur (Indonesia), Tri Agung Rooswiadji (Indonesia), (Sengthong Vongsakid (Laos), Ian G. Baird and Somphong Bounphasy (Laos), Malina Soning (Malaysia), Thomas Jalong (Malaysia), Neal Nirmal (Malaysia), Arsenio Tanchuling (Philippines), Ben Malayang III (Philippines), David de Vera (Philippines), Pinkaew Laungaramsri (Thailand), Jaruwan Kaewmahanin (Thailand) and Pisit Charnsnoh (Thailand).

- **a regional review of Community Conserved Areas and Co-managed Protected Areas in the Horn of Africa by Marco Bassi** (Italy) – with contributions from Boku Tache (Ethiopia), Abdurahiman Kubsa (Ethiopia), Luke Quentin (Kenya) and Guyo Hassan (Kenya) and with the advice of Ed Barrow (Kenya).

- **a review of Community Conserved Areas and Co-managed Protected Areas in Brazil by Claudio Carrera Maretti** (Brazil) – with contributions from Wanda Maldonado (Brazil), José Carlos Carvalho (Brazil), José Pedro de Oliveira Costa (Brazil), Marco Antônio Ramos Caminha (Brazil), Julio Gonchorosky (Brazil), Atanagildo de Deus Matos (Brazil), José Juarez Leitão dos Santos (Brazil), Rosely Alvim Sanches, (Brazil), João Paulo Capobianco (Brazil), Fany Ricardo (Brazil), Francisco de Sales Coutinho (Brazil), Carlos C. Martins Leal (Brazil), Joaquim de Souza Belo (Brazil), Humberto Candeias Cavalcanti (Brazil) and Manuel Mercado Soares (Brazil).

- **a regional review of Community Conserved Areas and Co-managed Protected Areas (focusing on terrestrial and non indigenous protected areas) in Central America by Vivienne Solís Rivera** (Costa Rica), **Patricia Madrigal Cordero** (Costa Rica), **Ivannia Ayales Cruz** (Costa Rica), **Marvin Fonseca Borrás** (Costa Rica), **Felipe Matos Gonzáles** (Costa Rica) **and Alejandra Salazar Dreja** (Costa Rica) – with contributions from Thora Amend (Panamá), Nellie Catzim (Belize), Moreno Heron (Belize), Verna Samuels (Belize), Donald Campbell (Costa Rica), Georg Kiechle (Costa Rica), Javier Mulling (Costa Rica), Franklin Sequeira (Costa Rica), Rigoberto Vargas (Costa Rica), Silvia Chaves (Costa Rica/Panamá), Meivis Ortiz (Costa Rica/Panamá), Doribel Herrador (El Salvador), Ernesto Méndez (El Salvador), James R. Barborak (USA), Sandra Rangel (Guatemala), Ileana Valenzuela, (Guatemala), Enrique Alvarado (Honduras), Modesto Ochoa (Honduras), Ramón Ordoñez (Honduras), Ángel Mendoza Pinacho (México), Francisco Chapela Mendoza (México), Inti Escalona Lüttig (México), Leticia Merino Pérez (México), Lilia Pérez Santiago (México), Cristian Tovilla Hernández (México), Roberto Iván Aguilar (Nicaragua), Edgar Castañeda (Nicaragua), Carol Chávez (Nicaragua), Carlos A. Rivas (Nicaragua), Ninoska Rivera (Nicaragua), Ventura Abrego (Panamá), Geodisio Castillo (Panamá), Melquiades Cedeño (Panamá), Arnoldo De León (Panamá), Fernando Domínguez (Panamá), Jorge Faisal Mosquera, (Panamá), Daniel Holness (Panamá), Michel La Forge (Panamá), Meky Morales (Panamá), Alfonso Sanabria (Panamá) and Ruby Zambrano (Panamá).

- **a regional review of Community Conserved Areas and Co-managed Protected Areas (focusing on marine and coastal and indigenous protected areas) in Central America by Hugh Govan** (Costa Rica) – with contributions from Adalberto Padilla (Honduras), Amilcar Castañeda Cortez (Costa Rica/Peru), Andy Caballero (Sint Maarten), Concepción Guevara (El Salvador), Deidamia Arjona (Panama), Emilio Ochoa (Ecuador), Fernando Palacios (Nicaragua), Fernando Simal (Bonaire), Geodisio Castillo (Panama), Greg Choc (Belice), Guillermo Garcia (Cuba), Gustavo Arencibia (Cuba), James Barborak (USA), Johann Krug (Panama), John Munro (British Virgin Islands), Jorg Grunberg (Guatemala/Nicaragua), Jorge Ventocilla (Panama), Juan Carlos Sueiro (Peru), Juan Llanes (Cuba), Julia Fraga (Mexico), Kay Lynn Plummer (St. Eustatius), Kelvin Guerrero (Republica Dominicana), Leda Menendez (Cuba), Leida Buglass

(Republica Dominicana), Luis Tenorio (Costa Rica), Marcos Williamson (Nicaragua), Mario Gonzalez Martin (Cuba), Marsha Kellogg (USA), Martin Bush (Haiti), Miguel Martinez (Guatemala), Mito Paz (Belize), Patricia Lamelas (Republica Dominicana), Patrick McConney (Barbados), Pedro Alcolado (Cuba), Peter Espeut (Jamaica), Rafael Puga (Cuba), Ratana Chuenpagdee (USA), Ricardo Soto (Costa Rica), Robert Pomeroy (USA), Robin Mahon (Grenadines), Stephen C. Jameson (Jamaica), Tania Crespo (Cuba), Valdemar Andrade (Belice), Violeta Reyna (Guatemala), Wil Maheia (Belice) and Yves Renard (Saint Lucia).

- **a regional review of Community Conserved Areas and Co-managed Protected Areas in Central Africa by John Nelson and Norbert Gami** – with contributions from Emmanuel Mve Mebia (Gabon), Leonard Usongo (Cameroon), Pierre Kakule Vwirasihikya (DRC), Ymua B M'keyo (DRC), Godefroid Kayungura Tasinzanzu (DRC), Chantal Shalukoma (DRC), Penninah Zaninka (Uganda), Jerome Lewis (UK), Bertin Tchikangwa (Cameroon), Samuel Nguiffo (Cameroon), Paluku Vasangrolo Pavasa (Cameroon), Laurent Some (Cameroon), Benoit Ndameau (Cameroon), Rynaer Tichmayer (Cameroon), Henri Nleme (Cameroon), Emmanuel Minsolo (Cameroon), Ernest Adjina (Cameroon), Prosper Mbe (Cameroon) and Germain Ngandul (Cameroon).

- **a regional review of Community Conserved Areas and Co-managed Protected Areas in Southern Africa by Webster Whande, Tembela Kepe and Marshall Murphree** – including specially-prepared papers by Brian Child (Zimbabwe), Brian Jones (Namibia), Cecil Machena (Zimbabwe), Rowan Martin (Zimbabwe) and James Murombedzi (Zimbabwe).

- **a paper on the history of conservation by Ken MacDonald** (USA).

- **two special issues of** *Parks*, **the journal of WCPA, on Local Communities and Protected Areas** (no. 12(2): 101pp., 2002, edited by Jessica Brown and Ashish Kothari) and on **Conservation Partnerships in Africa** (no. 13(1): 79pp., edited by Grazia Borrini-Feyerabend and Trevor Sandwith).

- **two special issues of** *Policy Matters*, the journal of CEESP, on **Sustainable Livelihoods and Co-management of Natural Resources** (no. 10, 147pp., 2002, edited by Grazia Borrini-Feyerabend and Taghi Farvar) and on **Community Empowerment for Conservation** (no. 12, 320pp., September 2003, edited by Grazia Borrini-Feyerabend, Alex de Sherbinin, Chimère Diaw, Gonzalo Oviedo and Diane Pansky).

- Other documents that provided very useful insights in the development of the Guidelines, such as a paper on the paradigm shift for protected areas by **Adrian Phillips**, papers on CCAs and CMPAs by **Dermot Smyth** (Australia), **Jean Paul Gladu** (Canada) and Andy Inglis (Scotland), an edited volume on innovative governance for protected areas edited by **Hanna Jaireth and Dermoth Smyth** (Australia), a paper on institutional change as related to protected areas by **Janis Alcorn** (USA), papers on indigenous people and protected areas issues by **Marcus Colchester** (UK) and **Fergus MacKay** (UK), a presentation on co-management of protected areas in Romania by **Erika Stanciu** (Romania), a draft paper on issues of culture and conservation by **Peter Simonic and Božidar Jezernik** (Slovenia) and a partial synthesis of information by **Andres Luque** (Colombia) and **Charles Brunton** (USA) in consultation with Lisbet Kugler (USA) and Gordon Geballe (USA).

Most of the TILCEPA and CMWG work has been carried out on a volunteer basis. Partial support for the production of the above mentioned reviews, papers and special issues of journals was generously provided by a grant from **Sida – the Swedish Development Cooperation Agency** through the **EPP project implemented by the World Resources Institute** (WRI) and the IUCN World Commission on Protected Areas. Office and communication support was provided by the **Collaborative Management Working Group (CMWG) of CEESP**. The publication of this volume is possible because of a grant from the **Global Environment Facility (GEF)** through the United Nations Environmental Programme (UNEP), as part of support to the preparation and follow up to the 2003 World Parks Congress in Durban (South Africa). Finally, like all the publications in the series, the Guidelines are produced with the unfailing support of the University of Cardiff.

This work is dedicated to the memory of **Mady Abdhoulanzis (Madagascar), Omar Asghar Khan (Pakistan), Chico Mendez (Brazil), Steve Szabo (Australia) and Norbert Zongo (Burkina Faso)**. Much of their lives were dedicated to ensuring the conditions for community livelihoods in harmony with conservation. May the respect, intelligence and care with which they crafted their work inspire many others.

Grazia Borrini-Feyerabend, Ashish Kothari and Gonzalo Oviedo

Acronyms

ALMP	Ancestral Land Management Plan
CADC	Certificate of Ancestral Domain Claim
CADT	Certificate of Ancestral Domain Title
CBD	Convention on Biological Diversity
CCA	Community Conserved Area
CEESP	Commission on Environmental, Economic and Social Policy
CFSA	Community Forest Stewardship Agreement
CMPA	Co-Managed Protected Area
CMWG	Collaborative Management Working Group
EPP	Ecosystems, Protected Areas and Peoples
GIS	Geographical Information System
ILO	International Labour Organization
IMA	Inter-institutional Management Authority
IPA	Indigenous Protected Area
NIPAS	National Integrated Protected Area System
NRM	Natural Resource Management
NTFP	Non-Timber Forest Products
PA	Protected Area
PMB	Participatory Management Board
Sida	Swedish International Development Cooperation Agency
TCO	Territorio Comunitario de Origen
TILCEPA	Theme on Indigenous and Local Communities, Equity and Protected Areas
UDHR	Universal Declaration of Human Rights
UNEP	United Nations Environment Programme
UNHCR	United Nations High Commissioner for Refugees
WCC	World Conservation Congress
WCPA	World Commission on Protected Areas
WRI	World Resources Institute
WWF	World Wide Fund for Nature (World Wildlife Fund in the USA and Canada)

Introduction

Throughout the world, managing protected areas involves people and organizations in widely differing roles. Field managers, whether working for an agency or for a community, deal with concrete problems and responsibilities on a daily basis and directly enjoy the rewards that only nature and culture at their best are able to provide. Local authorities and residents – administrators, community members, landowners and businesses – "live with" the protected areas, face restrictions, harness benefits and are variously involved in relevant concerns and decision making. Agency managers at the national level are concerned with systems of protected areas and the conservation benefits they provide as a whole; they, in turn, are accountable to the general public and taxpayers for official expenditure on protected areas. Natural and social scientists, and conservation and human rights advocates engage in understanding and refining management options and practices. And policy makers and legislators at the national and international level help shape the overall context in which protected areas exist.

For many of the above-mentioned managers, the issue that is often of greatest concern is how protected areas relate to local people – most importantly indigenous peoples and local and mobile communities.[1] This volume in the Best Practice Guideline Series has been designed to offer them ideas and concrete advice on ways to enhance the equity of that relationship, and to make it work better for conservation. The following audiences have been kept particularly in mind:

- staff of protected area agencies at all levels, whether working at national or site level;

- staff of conservation or development NGOs, whether working at international, national or site levels;

- community leaders;

- local conservation committees;

- policy makers and legislators who shape the framework for protected areas.

Conventional protected area approaches dominant over the past 100 to 150 years have tended to see people and nature as separate entities, often requiring the exclusion of human communities from areas of interest, prohibiting their use of natural resources and seeing their concerns as incompatible with conservation. While some kinds of protected areas (e.g. those corresponding to IUCN categories V and VI[2]) are assumed to accommodate human communities, more prestige seems to have been attached to those designed to exclude them both as residents and decision-makers (usually corresponding to IUCN categories I, II and III). Since *most* protected areas in the world have people residing within them or dependent on them for their livelihoods, the conventional exclusionary approaches have engendered profound social costs. This is particularly true when the

---

[1] While we recognise the critical difference between indigenous peoples and local and mobile communities, in this volume we have often used the term "communities" to denote all of them, for the sake of convenience.

[2] IUCN *et al.*, 1994.

affected indigenous peoples and local communities were already, even before the protected area intervention, among the most marginalized groups.

These Guidelines explore protected area approaches and models that see conservation as fully compatible with human communities – as managers, decision-makers, residents, users, caretaking neighbours – and that regard such communities as an asset to conservation rather than a liability. Drawing on recent experience and best practice from around the world, as well as from reflections and guidance developed at the local, national, regional and international levels, these Guidelines offer considerations, concepts and ideas. They do not prescribe blueprint solutions, but offer a menu of options for action, to be reviewed by the concerned actors and adapted to their circumstances.

The structure of these Guidelines is as follows:

- **Chapters 1 and 2** summarise the **background necessary to understand** the evolving relationship between communities and protected areas (they do not contain practical advice);

- **Chapter 3** assists the reader to carry out a very brief "**situation analysis**" and identify, among the chapters that follow, those most likely to respond to their concerns and expected professional tasks. Table 3.1, in particular, acts as "signpost" to help readers find the parts of the text most relevant to them.

- **Chapter 4** deals with **Co-managed Protected Areas**. These are protected areas established by or with the approval of governments and subjected to co-management regimes involving indigenous peoples and local and mobile communities. The chapter offers four sets of *options for action* to improve both equity and conservation in official protected areas.

- **Chapter 5** describes the concept and practice of **Community Conserved Areas**. It illustrates characteristics and common features of protected environments and resources established and managed by indigenous peoples and local and mobile communities. The chapter offers five sets of *options for action* by which Community Conserved Areas can be "recognised" and supported towards enhanced equity and conservation.

- **Chapter 6** speaks to professionals working at national and international levels and is concerned with the **overall policy context for protected areas**. It offers four broad sets of *policy options*, coherent with and supportive of the *options for*

Two key definitions used in these Guidelines

Co-managed Protected Area
Government-designated protected area where decision making power, responsibility and accountability are shared between governmental agencies and other stakeholders, in particular the indigenous peoples and local and mobile communities that depend on that area culturally and/or for their livelihoods

Community Conserved Area
Natural and modified ecosystems, including significant biodiversity, ecological services and cultural values, voluntarily conserved by indigenous peoples and local and mobile communities through customary laws or other effective means

---

action described in Chapters 4 and 5 and allowing the full contributions of indigenous and local communities to unfold.

This volume builds upon the IUCN's efforts to pursue equity in conservation in the decade since the term was first included in the IUCN mission statement[3] and upon the work of the IUCN Theme on Indigenous and Local Communities, Equity and Protected Areas (TILCEPA) – a joint Theme of the CEESP and WCPA Commissions. Much of this work was done in preparation for the Vth World Parks Congress in Durban (South Africa), September 2003.[4] The Guidelines also draw upon the outputs of that Congress and on the Programme of Work on Protected Areas approved by the 7th Conference of Parties to the Convention on Biological Diversity in February 2004 (CBD/COP7). As these were shaped by both government agencies and representatives of indigenous people, mobile indigenous peoples and local communities, we hope that this volume reflects at least in part their aspirations and concerns.

---

[3]   IUCN General Assembly Resolution 19.1 (January 1994).

[4]   See the Acknowledgment section. This preparatory work was supported by the Ecosystems, Protected Areas and People project; the relevant papers, regional reviews and overall synthesis can be consulted at www.iucn.org/themes/ceesp/Wkg_grp/TILCEPA/community.htm.

1. A new understanding of protected areas

Protected areas represent the heart of the world's political and economic commitment to conserve biodiversity and other natural and related cultural resources. They are, therefore, a major component of official conservation policy and practice. On the basis of national returns, the United Nations Environment Programme's World Conservation Monitoring Centre (UNEP-WCMC) has recently calculated that there are more than 102,000 protected areas throughout the world. Taken together, they cover more than 11.5% of the terrestrial surface of the earth (though only 3.4% of the entire surface, since there are relatively few marine protected areas).[5] These sites have been established by virtually all countries of the world and are managed through special rules and for conservation goals. Conservation approaches, however, are evolving rapidly, responding to social and economic changes as well as advances in natural and social sciences. What is now being encouraged in international guidance for protected area policy and practice? What requires adaptation to new situations and challenges? International definitions provide a useful starting point for this analysis.

IUCN[6] defines a 'protected area' as: *"an area of land and/or sea especially dedicated to the protection and maintenance of biological diversity, and of natural and associated cultural resources, and managed through legal or other effective means"*. The CBD defines it as *"a geographically defined area which is designated or regulated and managed to achieve specific conservation objectives"*. The two definitions are not in conflict, although the IUCN one refers more directly to the economic ("resources") and cultural aspects of conservation (for a further discussion of the bearing of this on Community Conserved Areas, see Chapters 2 and 5).

Since the 1972 UN Conference on the Human Environment held at Stockholm, and even more since the 1992 UN Conference on Environment and Development of Rio, international and national approaches to conservation have had to harmonise with social needs and the development agenda. Thus the very perception of a protected area has evolved. The aims of protected areas now include the sustainable use of natural resources, the preservation of ecosystem services and integration with broader social development processes, along with the core role of biodiversity conservation. More attention is now given to respecting cultural values as essential associates of biodiversity (made explicit in the 1994 IUCN definition of a protected area) and to the need to involve indigenous and local communities in management decisions affecting them. Starting from a focus on "nature" that basically excluded people, more and more protected area professionals today recognise natural resources, people and cultures as fundamentally interlinked.[7]

---

[5] Chape *et al.*, 2003. This covers all areas that meet the IUCN definition of a protected area and are held on the World Database for Protected Areas. See also Mulongoy and Chape, 2004.

[6] Definition included in *Guidelines for Protected Area Management Categories* (IUCN, 1994).

[7] West and Brechin, 1991; Stevens, 1997; Posey, 1998; Oviedo *et al.*, 2000; Phillips, 2002; Wilson, 2003.

Three main lines of thinking have converged to produce this new understanding of protected areas.

The first has been a broadening of perspective from the specific protected territory, area or resources to the surrounding context. This line of thinking lays emphasis on:

- Networks of protected areas, and connectivity within the networks.[8]

- The integration of protected areas in the broader landscape/seascape, and within the regional and national economy and policy.[9]

- Protected areas as one of the several components necessary for an effective regional or national conservation strategy.[10]

The second line of thinking has emerged from advances in ecological sciences beyond the concept of "equilibrium conditions" for ecosystems. It stresses that:

- Ecosystems are open, always subjected to a variety of influences from their surroundings and in a state of flux.[11]

- "Disturbances", such as grazing from herbivores or periodic fires, are extremely important in conservation efforts, and human disturbances that occur within ecological limits can be part of the dynamic pattern of conservation.[12]

- Ecosystem management is best understood as an adaptive process, strongly dependent on local biological history and context.[13]

Finally, a third line of thinking, derived from lessons learned in field practice, recommends to:

- Work with, rather than against, indigenous and local communities, NGOs, and the private sector, provided that all such actors are committed to basic conservation goals.[14]

- Develop management partnerships among social actors, benefiting from their complementary capacities and advantages.[15]

---

[8] Davey, 1998; Bennett, 1998; Boyd, 2004.

[9] See Forman and Godron, 1986; Lucas, 1992; Bennett, 1998; Beresford and Phillips, 2000; CBD Decision V/6 Ecosystem Approach, Nairobi, 2000; Turner *et al.*, 2001; and Ramsar Convention Secretariat, 2004.

[10] IUCN, UNEP and WWF, 1991; CBD, 1992; UNESCO, 1995.

[11] Whittaker and Levin, 1977; Fiedler and Jain, 1992. In addition, the dynamics of natural communities have multiple persistent states and "patch dynamics" and "shifting mosaics" are often necessary for the survival of species requiring multiple habitats (e.g. for shelter, forage, mating, etc.). See Pickett and Thompson, 1978; Bormann and Lickens, 1979; Luken, 1990.

[12] Mc Naughton, 1989; Fiedler and Jain, 1992; ICSU, 2002; Gunderson and Holling, 2002; MEA, 2003.

[13] Holling, 1978; www.for.gov.bc.ca/hfp/amhome/introgd/toc.htm; Gunderson and Pritchard, 2002.

[14] West and Brechin, 1991; CBD article 8(j), 1992 and subsequent decisions on implementation; Resolution 19.23 on the « Importance of community-based approaches » , IUCN General Assembly, 1994; Resolution 1.42 on « Collaborative Management for Conservation », World Conservation Congress, 1996; Kothari *et al.*, 1996; Borrini-Feyerabend, 1997; Ghimire and Pimbert, 1997; Beltran, 2000; Recommendations no. 5.24; 5.26 and 5.27 of the 5th World Parks Congress, 2003; Brechin *et al.*, 2003; CBD, 2004.

[15] McMcNeely, 1995; Borrini-Feyerabend, 1996; IUCN Resolution 1.42 (Montreal, 1996); Kothari *et al.*, 1998; Stolton and Dudley, 1999; IUCN Resolution 2.15 (Amman, 2000); Kothari *et al.*, 2000; Borrini-Feyerabend *et al.*, 2004 [in press].

■ Perceive the conservation of biodiversity as inseparable from its sustainable use and the fair sharing of the benefits arising from the utilization of genetic resources, as reflected in the three main objectives of the CBD.[16]

If we juxtapose the conventional and the emerging approach to protected area management, a change of perspectives occurs that Phillips (2003) has labelled a "paradigm shift" (see Table 1.1). The juxtaposition should not be read to mean that all protected areas used to be managed according to the "conventional model" and now are, or soon will be, managed according to the "new understanding" model. Far from it! As a matter of fact, much of the protected areas legislation developed in the 1970s and 1980s in many countries, as well as the style of many individual protected area managers since then, appears close to the principles and ideas embodied in the "new understanding" column. But the prevailing political context may not have allowed appropriate practice to unfold, and obstacles often arise in connection with land tenure and macro-economic policies, ethnic and political conflicts, and power inequities at various levels. In sum, Table 1.1 renders visible an average "pattern of change" that has notable exceptions, has been related to different constraints and opportunities and has been proceeding at a different pace and with different results in different contexts.

Table 1.1   A paradigm shift in protected area management
(adapted and expanded from Phillips, 2003)

The conventional understanding of protected areas	The emerging understanding of protected areas
Established as separate units	Planned as part of national, regional and international systems
Managed as "islands"	Managed as elements of networks (protected areas connected by "corridors", "stepping stones" and biodiverssity-friendly land uses)
Managed reactively, within a short timescale, with little regard to lessons from experience	Managed adaptively, on a long time perspective, taking advantage of on-going learning
About protection of existing natural and landscape assets – not about the restoration of lost values	About protection but also restoration and rehabilitation, so that lost or eroded values can be recovered
Set up and run for conservation (not for productive use) and scenic protection (not ecosystem functioning)	Set up and run for conservation but also for scientific, socio-economic (including the maintenance of ecosystem services) and cultural objectives
Established in a technocratic way	Established as a political act, requiring sensitivity, consultations and astute judgment
Managed by natural scientists and natural resource experts	Managed by multi-skilled individuals, including some with social skills
Established and managed as a means to control the activities of local people, without regard to their needs and without their involvement	Established and run with, for, and in some cases by local people; sensitive to the concerns of local communities (who are empowered as participants in decision making)

---

[16]   CDB, Article 1.

Table 1.1   A paradigm shift in protected area management (cont.)

Run by central government	Run by many partners, including different tiers of government, local communities, indigenous groups, the private sector, NGOs and others
Paid for by taxpayers	Paid for from many sources and, as much as possible, self-sustaining
Benefits of conservation assumed as self-evident	Benefits of conservation evaluated and quantified
Benefiting primarily visitors and tourists	Benefiting primarily the local communities who assume the opportunity costs of conservation
Viewed as an asset for which national considerations prevail over local ones	Viewed as a community heritage as well as a national asset

Conservation and equity

Underlying several elements of the changing perspective on protected areas is a new concern for social equity in conservation. This is driven by practical considerations (in many circumstances conservation cannot and will not happen without the support of the relevant communities)[17] but also by more widely shared ethical and moral concerns.[18] There is ample field-based evidence that conventional conservation initiatives have harmed many communities, including some among the world's poorest and most marginalized. Thus, some communities have been expelled from newly protected territories and involuntarily resettled, with sometimes appalling socio-cultural and economic consequences. Some traditionally mobile communities have been forced against their wishes to abandon their nomadic existence and adopt a sedentary lifestyle, with similarly tragic results, including for the ecology of the settlement areas. Communities in many countries have been disrupted and impoverished by being forced to abandon the use of resources upon which their livelihoods depended – action often taken without any redress through compensation (see an example in Box 1.1). And communities have been dis-empowered when their erstwhile control over lands and resources has been taken over by governments or by private corporations. Indigenous peoples, mobile indigenous peoples and local communities have campaigned for decades about these problems, but many in the conservation establishment have rejected their claims. Now that the international policy circles are, at least in theory, committed to the eradication of poverty,[19] this position is no longer defensible: it would make little sense to set up poverty-eradication programmes alongside conservation initiatives that result in greater poverty.[20]

---

[17]   IUCN Resolution 1.35, adopted at the First World Conservation Congress in Montreal, 1996, requests all states, agencies and organizations to adopt policies that "recognise that protected areas will survive only if they are seen to be of value, in the widest sense, to the nation as a whole and to local people in particular".

[18]   Brockington, 2003. Brockington argues that some government-run protected areas can remain effective or at least sustain their presence despite being managed and run in inequitable ways, and despite causing the impoverishment of communities. He thus argues that equity should be taken as a concern on a par with conservation not only for pragmatic reasons ("equity is good for conservation"), but also for ethical/ moral reasons ("equity is good *per se*").

[19]   "We will spare no effort to free our fellow men, women and children from the abject dehumanising conditions of extreme poverty to which more than a billion of them are currently subjected" (United Nations Millennium Declaration, September 2000).

Box 1.1   The Karrayu and the Awash National Park, Ethiopia
(adapted from Bassi, 2003)

The Karrayu are an Oromo pastoral group living in the upper Awash Valley, in the Northern section of the Rift Valley. Traditionally they have been living in and using three ecological zones: *ona ganna* a open grassland around Fontalle volcano used as a summer wet season grazing zone, *ona birraa* a riverine strand of land along the Awash river, used as autumn dry season grazing zone and including more than 15 holy grounds, and *ona bona*, a winter dry season grazing zone of shrubs and grassland between the two.

From the 1950s onwards Karrayu land was leased by the government to private enterprises for sugar production and, later on, a growing portion of riverine land has been developed into irrigated schemes for commercial agriculture. Workers and farmers migrated into the area, while the Karrayu lost their dry season pastures. In 1969 a hunting reserve was gazetted as National Park. The Karrayu and their northern neighbours, the Afar pastoralists, were displaced from an area of about 76,000 hectares, most of it in the critical *ona bona* and *ona birra* grazing area, with little compensation. It was estimated that the Karrayu have been squeezed from 150,000 to 60,000 hectares, remaining with the marginal *ona ganna* ecological zone. The rotational graze use pattern was forcedly broken, producing serious ecological degradation on the remaining part, outside the national park boundaries.

Because of dire need, both the Karrayu and the displaced clans of the Afar are periodically forced to lead their herds into the park's boundaries, which causes harsh conflicts with the park's management. Shooting between the park guards and the pastoralists, and between the Afar and Karrayu pastoralists competing for the remaining pastoral resources, is taking place with alarming frequency. Pastoral life has basically become unsustainable and many Karrayu families take up farming in unsuitable land or at the margin of the irrigated schemes. Having entirely lost access to their ceremonial grounds along the Awash rivers, they have all converted to Islam.

The Karrayu are caught in a permanent food crisis. The debate between the park's management and the representatives of pastoralists has so far focused on water points for pastoral use, with no agreements to date. Meanwhile, commercial farming is expanding inside the park's boundaries. The area has great potential for tourism, including a volcano, a hot spring and wildlife. It also had immense potential for a co-management agreement that would build upon the sacred grounds and management practices of the autochthonous resource users, regulate grazing to support livelihoods and maintain the habitat for wildlife. But, as the values and practices of the Karrayu are being eroded, a whole potential for conservation is being squandered as well.

For IUCN, the obligation to embrace equity is rooted in its mission – "to influence, encourage and assist societies throughout the world to conserve the integrity and diversity of nature and to ensure that any use of natural resources is *equitable* and ecologically sustainable" – and its vision: "a *just* world that values and conserves nature". But what does that mean, in practice?

At very least it means that *conservation should do no harm to human societies –* although it may require trade-offs – and that, whenever possible, it should provide benefits to the communities and people directly concerned. More broadly, a concern for social equity in conservation covers a range of issues, from human rights to sustainable

---

[20]   Cernea and Schmidt-Soltau, 2003.

use of natural resources, from participation of civil society to gender fairness. Such concerns may have been held by some within conservation circles for a number of years, but their impact on policy has been quite recent. It has, however, been rapid, as is evident in the decisions and actions of IUCN.

In 1991, *Caring for the Earth: A Strategy for Sustainable Living*, published by IUCN, WWF and UNEP, recommended:

- citizen involvement in establishing and reviewing national protected areas policy;

- the effective participation of local communities in the design, management and operation of individual protected areas;

- a sustainable economic return from protected areas, making sure that much of this goes to manage the area and supports local communities;

- that local communities, especially communities of indigenous peoples, and private organizations should establish and manage protected areas within the national system;

- that the protected areas do not become oases of diversity in a desert of uniformity, by providing for their integration within policies for the management of surrounding lands and waters.

Since then, IUCN has moved from rhetorical policy statements that focused on "assessing, controlling and convincing"[21] to more concrete position statements on sustainable development, sustainable use,[22] social equity,[23] and gender equity,[24] as well as to adopting resolutions on the rights of indigenous peoples[25] and participatory approaches[26] to conservation. Several of these have also been developed by IUCN into technical advice.[27]

---

[21] Larsen, 2003.

[22] IUCN World Conservation Congress Resolution 2.29 (Montreal, 1996) (the IUCN Policy Statement on Sustainable Use of Wild Living Resources) noted the need to mainstream the concept in all IUCN activities. The resolution underlines that " Use, if sustainable, can serve human needs on an ongoing basis while contributing to the conservation of biological diversity". The CBD reinforces this approach, linking sustainable use, incentive mechanisms and the knowledge, innovations and practices of indigenous and local communities.

[23] The IUCN Policy on Social Equity (2000) states that "IUCN understands that to be able to design effective programmes that promote sustainable and equitable conservation and natural resources use, it has to fully embrace socioeconomic and cultural equity concerns in its policies, programmes and projects at the local, national, regional and global level".

[24] IUCN, 1998.

[25] In 1990, IUCN General Assembly Resolution 18.17 requested that IUCN advice should integrate population characteristics « from the point of view of sustainable use and management but also the quality of human life as defined in the Universal Declaration of Human Rights and the World Health Organization's definition of health ».

[26] Caring for the Earth calls for "full participation", raises a number of guiding principles and underlines the importance of community-driven processes. Following the UN Conference on Environment and Development (1992), IUCN General Assembly Recommendation 19.22 urged all states and local authorities to: "ensure fully the public participation by local people and indigenous peoples in decisions concerning the planning, development and management of national parks and other protected areas, and to provide that their interests are treated equitably and are fully respected by all authorities and agencies with responsibility in or impacting on national parks and other protected areas". IUCN World Conservation Congress Resolution 1.43 on "public participation and the right to know" reiterates earlier commitments through Agenda 21 and underlines the need for legally binding measures to guarantee public participation, access to information and access to justice. Later, the call for public participation was consolidated through international, regional and national processes. More specific calls for collaborative management of natural resources are included in IUCN World Conservation Congress Resolution 1.42 (Montreal, 1996) and Resolution 2.15 (Amman, 2000).

The rights of indigenous peoples and of local and mobile communities

Attention to the rights of indigenous and local communities in protected area management is relatively recent. In the nineteen and twentieth centuries, many protected areas were established on land and resources held in common property by communities but perceived as *terra nullius* (nobody's property) when it came to asking permission, offering compensation and the like. The resident peoples were often expelled or severely restricted in terms of permissible uses of natural resources, often without compensation. Today, few people argue against the need to engage positively with resident or neighbouring communities in protected area management, and probably no-one would defend the proposition that human rights are less important in relation to protected areas than elsewhere. Moreover, around the world conservation agencies and communities are also "learning by doing" in an enormous variety of specific situations, trying to understand and apply an evolving body of international and national laws and regulations on the rights of indigenous peoples and local communities.

The emergence of "human rights" as a subject of global policy is itself a relatively recent development. It first found expression in the aftermath of World War II, in the 1948 Universal Declaration of Human Rights. Since then, numerous international agreements have sought to translate the lofty ethical principles and values that serve as the foundation of human rights into practical obligations for "minimal standards" when dealing with people in general and vulnerable groups and individuals in particular. In this sense, recognising and respecting these rights is seen as the minimum standard obligations, and violating rights as breaching these obligations.

The International Covenant on Economic, Social and Cultural Rights, which was adopted in 1966 and came into force ten years later, outlined rights in specific terms. It introduced a number of human rights processes (ranging from monitoring procedures[28] to global summits), and required governments to implement its provisions. The specific concerns about the rights of indigenous peoples have emerged as part of this evolving body of human rights. Thus the ILO Convention No. 169 Concerning Indigenous and Tribal Peoples in Independent Countries, adopted in 1989, defines Indigenous Peoples (see Box 1.2) and recognises their rights to have their social, cultural, religious and spiritual values and practices recognised and protected (Art. 5) and the right to define their development priorities (Art. 7). It affirms indigenous peoples' rights to lands traditionally occupied by them *in toto* or in part and stresses that particular attention should be paid to the situation of nomadic peoples and shifting cultivators. Article 15 states that indigenous peoples should participate in the use, management and conservation of renewable and non-renewable natural resources. Article 16 states that indigenous peoples shall not be removed from the lands that they occupy and, if this is necessary as an exceptional measure, relocation shall take place only with their free and informed consent and with assured right of return and proper compensation. Further elaborations are provided by the Draft

[27]   See Borrini-Feyerabend, 1996; Beltrán (Ed.), 2000.

[28]   www.unhchr.ch.

United Nations Declaration on the Rights of Indigenous Peoples, which, although not yet adopted, provides much useful advice.[29]

While there is an international trend to recognise the collective rights of indigenous peoples, the rights of local communities have generally received less attention. Box 1.3 offers a definition of local communities, many of which have extended residence in a given environment, a rich tradition in their relationship with the land and the natural resources, well-established customary tenure and use practices, effective management institutions and a direct dependence on the resources for their livelihoods and cultural identity. They too claim "rights" to their land and natural resources. The concept of Community Property Rights has been proposed to address such rights, encompassing terrestrial resources as well as coastal and marine resources and certain governments have begun enshrining these kinds of rights into national law. In the Philippines, for instance, an administrative order calls for the delineation and

---

Box 1.2   Indigenous peoples

In its policies on indigenous peoples, IUCN uses the definition or "statement of coverage" contained in the ILO Convention 169 on Indigenous and Tribal Peoples in Independent Countries.[30]

According to that Convention, *indigenous peoples* include:

- *tribal peoples in independent countries whose social, cultural, and economic conditions distinguish them from other sections of the national community, and whose status is regulated wholly or partially by their own customs or traditions or by special laws or regulations;*

- *peoples in independent countries who are regarded as indigenous on account of their descent from the populations which inhabited the country, or a geographical region to which the country belongs, at the time of conquest or colonisation or the establishment of present state boundaries and who, irrespective of their legal status, retain some or all of their own social, economic, cultural and political institutions.*

Also according to the Convention, self-identification as indigenous or tribal shall be regarded as a fundamental criterion for determining the groups to which the provisions of the Convention apply. Among the criteria used by indigenous peoples to identify themselves as such are: their own historical continuity with pre-colonial societies, the close relationship with the land and natural resources of their own territory, their peculiar socio-political system, their own language, culture, values and beliefs, not belonging to the dominant sectors of their national society and seeing themselves as different from it.

---

[29]   The Draft Declaration stresses the self determination of indigenous peoples and their right to live in freedom, peace and security as distinct peoples, on their lands or territories, while preserving cultural traditions and languages. While the text is still under development, the draft emphasises the rights of those practicing cultural traditions and customs, including the spiritual and material relationships they have with the lands and other resources which they have traditionally owned, occupied or used. It also calls for the restitution of their rights where lands, territories and resources were confiscated, occupied, used or damaged without free and informed consent, and for the full recognition of cultural and intellectual property rights. Issues of compensation for land and property taken away by settler societies are an important concern and still a source of debate. IUCN Resolution WCC 1.49 IUCN called on its members to "comply with the spirit of the draft UN Declaration on the Rights of Indigenous Peoples", and several other Resolutions indicate that IUCN frames its policy on indigenous peoples on the principles of the draft UN Declaration on the Rights of Indigenous Peoples (e.g. Resolutions WCC 1.49, 1.50, 1.51, 1.52, 1.54 and 1.55).

[30]   Oviedo, 2003b.

mapping of municipal coastal waters, which should be the priority fishing grounds of small scale artisan fishermen.[31]

Among international conventions and provisions on the conservation of natural resources, some have specific relevance for equity and the rights of both indigenous and local communities:

- Resolution VII.8 on Local Communities and Indigenous People, adopted by the Conference of the Parties to the Ramsar Convention (San José, 1999)[32] and related Guidelines for Establishing and Strengthening Local Communities' and Indigenous People's Participation in the Management of Wetlands (also adopted by the Convention),[33] recognise that indigenous people and local communities "*have*

Box 1.3   Local communities

A community is a human group sharing a territory and involved in different but related aspects of livelihoods—such as managing natural resources, producing knowledge and culture, and developing productive technologies and practices.[34] Since this definition can apply to a range of sizes (is a city a community? is the sum of all people inhabiting a watershed a community?), it can be further specified that the members of a "*local* community" are those people that are likely to have *face-to-face* encounters and/or *direct* mutual influences in their daily life. In this sense, a rural village, a clan in transhumance or the inhabitants of an urban neighbourhood can be considered a "local community", but not all the inhabitants of a district, a city quarter or even a rural town. A local community could be permanently settled or mobile.

Most communities have developed their identity and cultural characteristics over time by devising and applying a strategy to cope with a given environment and manage its natural resources. They possess a distinctive form of social organization, and their members share in varying degrees political, economic, social and cultural characteristics (in particular language, behavioural norms, values, aspirations and often also health and disease patterns). They also function, or have functioned in the past, as micro-political bodies with specific capacities and authority.

Important processes in community life comprise social integration (cooperation to address common needs), social conflict (clashing of needs and wants among individual members or families within the community), cultural continuity and cultural change. Mechanisms that generally promote integration in communities include patterns of reciprocity (such as exchanges in marriages or economic trade) and redistribution (sharing economic surpluses among individuals or families). Conditions that may promote conflict in communities include major differences in power and status, e.g. among the young and the elderly, men and women, or among different community units (households) or sub-groups (clans, classes, occupational groups, castes, interest associations, etc.). Such differences are usually reflected in different access to resources (land, capital, water, trees, services, etc.), sometimes leading to exploitation (getting more than others in a common activity), accumulation (avoiding the sharing of surpluses) and the possible splitting or break-down of communities.

In order to survive and develop as a social body, a community continually manages a balance between the opposing forces of conflict and integration, continuity and change. The capacity of a community to deal with these phenomena through time can be used as a criterion

---

[31]   Ferrari, 2003.

[32]   www.ramsar.org/key_res_vii.08e.htm.

[33]   www.ramsar.org/key_guide_indigenous.htm.

[34]   Adapted from Borrini, 1992.

long-standing rights, ancestral values, and traditional knowledge and institutions associated with their use of wetlands".

- Article 8(j) of the CBD advocates that its Contracting Parties "*respect, preserve and maintain the knowledge, innovations and practices of indigenous and local communities embodying traditional lifestyles relevant for the conservation and sustainable use of biological diversity*"; that they "*promote their wider application with the approval and involvement of the holders of such knowledge, innovations and practices*"; and that they "*encourage the equitable sharing of the benefits arising from the utilization of such knowledge, innovations and practices*". The CBD Programme of Work on Protected Areas approved in 2004 is another case in point and will be dealt with in Chapter 2.

Within IUCN, there has also been considerable policy development on issues of the rights of indigenous peoples and local and mobile communities in the context of conservation. As noted above, *Caring for the Earth* (1991) sought to move beyond participation and emphasised the importance of community-driven processes. More specifically, Action Recommendation 7.5 states: "*[All communities] should be encouraged by the governments to debate their environmental priorities and to develop local strategies (for example, through workshops involving invited experts). Governments should then help the communities to convert their strategies into action*". Then, after the fairly generic General Assembly Resolution 19.23 on the "Importance of Community-based Approaches" (Buenos Aires, 1994), a number of IUCN Resolutions and policy documents incrementally recognised community rights to land and resource access, ownership, participation in decision-making, tenure security and sustainable use.

Thus WCC Resolution 1.50 (Montreal, 1996) on "Indigenous Peoples, Intellectual Property Rights, and Biological Diversity" called for "*… respect for cultural diversity, including linguistic diversity, as a basic condition to maintain and protect indigenous knowledge […] establishment of a process which facilitates the recognition of indigenous peoples knowledge as the intellectual property of its holder […] recognition of the principle that use of the knowledge, innovations and practices of indigenous peoples and local communities be made with their approval and consultation, and that indigenous peoples and local communities share equitably in the benefits deriving from such use […] establishment of national policies to ensure the promotion, recovery, systematization and strengthening of indigenous knowledge related to biodiversity with the prior informed consent of the peoples concerned*".

WCC Resolution 1.53 on "Indigenous Peoples and Protected Areas" and Resolution 1.42 on "Collaborative Management for Conservation" advise members to recognise indigenous rights in conservation, establish co-management agreements and secure equitable benefit sharing.

Through its policy on social equity[35] the IUCN re-affirmed these aims and stressed the need to:

- "Recognise the social, economic and cultural rights of indigenous peoples such as their right to lands and territories and natural resources, respecting their social and cultural identity, their customs, traditions and institutions.

---

[35]   IUCN, 2000.

- Ensure full and just participation of indigenous peoples in all conservation activities supported and implemented by IUCN.

- Support indigenous peoples' right to make their own decisions affecting their lands, territories and resources.

- Promote gender equality and equity within conservation, and a more balanced relationship between women and men in the distribution of costs and benefits, access and control, and decision-making opportunities, over natural resources".

The policy statement from IUCN and WWF entitled Principles and Guidelines for Indigenous and Traditional Peoples and Protected Areas[36] states: "Indigenous and other traditional peoples have long associations with nature and [...] have made significant contributions to the maintenance of many of the earth's most fragile ecosystems [... and ...] there should be no inherent conflict between the objectives of protected areas and the existence, within and around their borders, of indigenous and other traditional peoples. [...] Agreements drawn up between conservation institutions, including protected area management agencies, and indigenous and other traditional peoples for the establishment and management of protected areas [...] should be based on full respect for the rights of indigenous and other traditional peoples to traditional, sustainable use of their lands, territories, waters, coastal seas and other resources. At the same time, such agreements should be based on the recognition by indigenous and other traditional peoples of their responsibility to conserve biodiversity, ecological integrity and natural resources harboured in those protected areas. [...] The principles of decentralization, participation, transparency and accountability should be taken into account in all matters pertaining to the mutual interests of protected areas and indigenous and other traditional peoples.[...] Indigenous and other traditional peoples should be able to share fully and equitably in the benefits associated with protected areas".

The IUCN and WWF principles and guidelines thus provide grounds—at least in reference to indigenous and traditional peoples—for an IUCN rights-based approach to conservation. Yet, the implementation of this approach has been so far slow and much remains to be done.[37] Encouragingly, numerous examples of indigenous peoples and local and mobile communities effectively involved in conservation illustrate in practice how conservation benefits and the respect of indigenous and community rights can co-exist in a synergistic way.[38]

Taking a human rights approach to protected area management involves addressing the current, cumulative and future impacts of protected areas on a broad set of rights, including self determination and the right to collective ownership of lands and natural resources. The fact that indigenous peoples and local and mobile communities are advocating collective rather than individual rights is of great importance for conservation. "(First), when applied to land, collective rights are the basis for maintaining the integrity of the territory and avoiding ecological fragmentation, which is in turn a key requirement for meaningful biodiversity conservation. Secondly, collective rights provide a strong basis for the

---

[36] Beltrán, 2000.

[37] MacKay, 2002.

[38] www.iucn.org/themes/ceesp/Wkg_grp/TILCEPA/community.htm. See also issues no. 12(2) and no.13 (1) of *Parks* and issues no. 10 and no. 12 of *Policy Matters*.

building and functioning of community institutions, which are indispensable for sound, long-term land and resource management. Thirdly, they strengthen the role of customary law as related to land management, and of traditional knowledge applied to broader territorial and landscape units."[39]

Rights and responsibilities

IUCN is not only concerned with rights – it also stresses accompanying community responsibilities. Thus, Resolution 1.44 on Public Access (Montreal, 1996) stresses that "the needs of conservation, management, ownership, safety and security may well require some limits on public access to land". Similar formulations run through several policy documents, such as the 1994 Protected Area Management Category Guidelines and the 2000 Principles and Guidelines for Indigenous and Traditional Peoples and Protected Areas. The governance stream at the 2003 World Parks Congress also amply stressed the need to recognise rights but at the same time associate them with responsibilities and accountability mechanisms.[40] The exercise of responsibilities means that any given body of natural resources needs to be perceived and dealt with as natural heritage *per se* and for the benefits of all generations. In this sense, a body of resources may not always be able to meet all the present local needs, and resource use may need to be restricted to reach particular conservation objectives. This matching of rights and responsibilities is crucial for conservation. The key question is how to assign responsibilities fairly and effectively – including restrictions in resource access and use – while maintaining an overall rights-based approach. The answer seems to lie in moving away from imposed restrictions to the participatory definition of, and agreement on, shared rules.

Management effectiveness

Along with the emergence of equity concerns in conservation, there has been a growing recognition of the unique knowledge, skills, resources and institutions that indigenous peoples and local and mobile communities can bring to protected area management. Management practices that engage communities are seen to enhance the long-term effectiveness of conservation.

The concept of "management effectiveness" has recently gained a foothold as part of the theory and practice of monitoring and evaluating protected areas. In this regard, the IUCN Management Effectiveness Guidelines[41] identify three main topics for evaluation:

- design issues relating to both individual sites and protected area systems;
- appropriateness of management systems and processes; and
- delivery of protected area objectives.

Thus, management effectiveness depends on good planning, good decision-making and good implementation of decisions. The interface with equity and the opportunity to

---

[39] Oviedo, 2003b.

[40] See www.iucn.org/themes/ceesp/Wkg_grp/TILCEPA/WPC/goverance%20final%20report%20Oct%2003.pdf.

[41] Hockings *et al.*, 2000.

elicit and harness the unique capacities of indigenous and local communities bear on all three of these. In other words, social concerns and capacities should be integrated into the design process, and civil society actors engaged as participants. Similar considerations arise in assessing the "appropriateness" of management systems and processes. And protected areas can be assessed for their capacity to deliver social benefits, including the protection of cultural diversity, as well as environmental objectives.

Equity advocates recommend planning in a participatory way and the setting-up of pluralist, co-management structures for decision-making and implementation. But how good and effective would participatory processes and structures be?[42] Would they not simply muddle and confuse the goals of conservation? Would not social benefits and community empowerment be in conflict with conservation benefits and "scientific" rigour?

While some commentators view participatory approaches with distrust, especially where strict protection measures appear necessary, others seek to develop solutions tailored to specific contexts, engaging the capacities of indigenous and local communities for conservation.[43] Documenting the conservation gains and failings of such experiences is the best way to provide meaningful and non-ideological answers to the questions asked above. An analysis of specific cases will help to determine if strict protection objectives can be compatible with community involvement in conservation, and to evaluate the conservation effectiveness of traditional practices, including area protection and resource use restriction imposed by communities themselves.[44] The relationship between the achievement of conservation objectives and the respect of human rights should also be explored and documented.

The IUCN Management Categories for Protected Areas

IUCN provides much advice on protected area management. The IUCN protected area management categories are a key instrument that IUCN recommends to facilitate communication about protected areas (IUCN, 1994a). The starting point is the IUCN definition of a protected area – *"an area of land and/or sea especially dedicated to the protection and maintenance of biological diversity, and of natural and associated cultural resources, and managed through legal or other effective means"*. Areas that meet that definition are then allocated to one of six management categories, *based upon the primary management objective of the area*. These categories are summarised in Table 1.2 (for a fuller explanation of objectives, criteria for selection, etc., see IUCN, 1994a).

---

[42] Worah, 2002.

[43] See for instance: Ralston *et al.*, 1983; Agarwal and Narain, 1989; Reader, 1990; Ghai and Vivian, 1992; Western and Wright, 1994; Pye-Smith and Borrini-Feyerabend, 1994;White *et al.*, 1994; Amend and Amend, 1995; McNeely, 1995; IUCN, 1996; Kothari *et al.*, 1997; Kothari *et al.*, 1998; Stolton and Dudley, 1999; IUCN/CEESP, 2002; IUCN/CEESP 2003.

[44] Sacred areas and resources in the landscape are often "known" to be uniquely rich in biodiversity, but it is less common to find studies that document and prove this to the satisfaction of conservationists.

Table 1.2   The IUCN protected areas management categories

Category Ia	Strict Nature Reserve: managed mainly for science.
Category Ib	Wilderness Area: managed mainly for wilderness protection.
Category II	National Park: managed mainly for ecosystem protection and recreation
Category III	Natural Monument: managed mainly for conservation of specific natural features
Category IV	Habitat/Species Management Area: managed mainly for conservation through management intervention
Category V	Protected Landscape/Seascape: managed mainly for landscape/seascape conservation and recreation
Category VI	Managed Resource Protected Area: managed mainly for the sustainable use of natural ecosystems

Although all protected areas must be "especially dedicated to the protection and maintenance of biological diversity, and of natural and associated cultural resources" the Guidelines for Protected Area Management Categories[45] recognise that the categories imply "a gradation of human intervention". Thus the detailed guidance on each category accepts that different level of human use and presence will occur, though in all cases these must be consistent with conservation and sustainability objectives. Thus, Category Ia should be "significantly free of human presence and capable of remaining so". The management of Category Ib can be compatible with "indigenous human communities living in low density and in balance with the available resources … ". Category II is to "take into account the needs of indigenous people". Category III is to deliver benefits to "any resident population". Category IV speaks of "delivering benefits to people living within the designated area". Category V underlines the importance of "the continuation of traditional uses, building practices and social and cultural manifestations" and includes " to bring benefits and contribute to the welfare of local communities" as a specific objective. Category VI is meant to conserve biodiversity while meeting community needs through a sustainable flow of natural products and services: it requires that at least two-thirds of the area be kept in a natural condition, and thus, in practice, limits the actual area in which community needs can be fulfilled to the one-third described as "limited areas of modified ecosystems".

A major piece of research on the categories was undertaken[46] between 2002 and 2004. This helped inform debate at the World Parks Congress. As a result, Recommendation 5.19 was adopted, which reaffirmed the definition of a protected area; stated that "in the application of the management categories IUCN's definition of a protected area[47] must always be met as the overarching criterion"; and confirmed that the "1994 system of protected area management categories, and in particular that the six category, objectives-based approach, should remain the essential foundation for the system". Without prejudice to these requirements, Recommendation 5.21 also called for a revised, up-dated edition of the 1994 guidelines, to be compiled through

---

[45]   IUCN, 1994a.

[46]   See Bishop *et al.*, [in print] and www.cf.ac.uk/cplan/sacl/.

[47]   The 1994 definition was restated in Recommendation 5.19.

an open, participatory process. This work, which should begin in 2005, should provide more extensive definitions and criteria and make more explicit the link between the categories and ecological networks, wider regional planning, sustainable livelihoods and the cultural and spiritual values the protected areas seek to conserve. The upcoming guidance should also include explicit reference to a governance dimension (see below), complementary to the categories, which should embrace the range of governance arrangements for protected areas, such as government-run, private protected areas and protected areas managed by indigenous and local communities.

In the case of Category V – Protected Landscapes/Seascapes – recently compiled guidance[48] is already available. These are areas where the interaction of people and nature through time has produced significant aesthetic, ecological or cultural values and, often, enhanced biological diversity. By definition, then, people are the primary stewards of these landscapes and should be supported in this role. As the architects of much that is valued, local people are the true managers of protected landscapes, perhaps even more so than the professionals who may be employed with that formal title.[49] Category V protected areas characteristically build on existing local tenure regimes (usually a mixture of property regimes) rather than relying on government ownership and control alone. This considerably expands the potential size of areas under conservation, and opens up new ways to plan and manage conservation.

It is important to stress that the IUCN protected area definition and associated management categories do not prescribe any type of ownership or management authority – they are "neutral" about these, so to speak.[50] This means that protected areas in any of the six categories can be owned and/or managed by communities, private parties, government authorities, NGOs or various combinations of these. Also, private ownership and customary community rights can coexist with the status of a protected area, although an official declaration may impose some restrictions and obligations.[51]

As to a human presence in protected areas, whether as residents or resource users, the IUCN protected area categories V and VI are conceived to be the most inclusive, and progressively greater restrictions on human activities normally apply in Categories IV–Ia. That said, there are examples of protected areas that achieve the objectives of each category alongside the presence of resident and user communities – though of course subject to appropriate limitations and restrictions (see Table 5.1 in Chapter 5). Furthermore, experience from around the world suggests that human communities living within or adjacent to protected areas can often serve as an *asset* to conservation rather than a liability.[52] This is *not a rule* and there are plenty of counterexamples – still less is it an argument for all protected areas to be opened to human access. But it does

---

[48] Phillips, 2002.

[49] On this, see both Phillips, 2002 and also Wilson, 2003. If the involvement of local people is essential, however, they are not the only source of expertise. Other stakeholders should also contribute and be taken into account.

[50] Borrini-Feyerabend, 2003.

[51] See WCC Resolution 1.33 on "Conservation on Community and privately-owned land and waters"; IUCN Principles and guidelines on indigenous and traditional peoples (Beltrán, 2000) as well as other guidance such as Guidelines for IUCN Category V Protected Areas (Phillips, 2002).

[52] Borrini-Feyerabend, 2004.

represent a new perspective on the relationship between people and protected areas, which has been endorsed by the Vth World Parks Congress and the 7th Conference of the Parties of the Convention on Biological Diversity. Both events called for a flexible approach to management rules for protected areas, carefully tailored to their ecological and social context.

2. The Vth World Parks Congress and the programme of work on protected areas of the Convention on Biological Diversity

Many of the substantial changes in the understanding of protected areas described in Chapter 1 acquired a clear articulation in the Durban Accord and Action Plan, and in the Recommendations developed at the Vth World Parks Congress of 2003, and, following that, in the Programme of Work on Protected Areas approved by the seventh Conference of the Parties of the CBD (CBD/COP 7) in February 2004.[53] The Durban Accord speaks of "forging a synergy" between conservation goals and "the interests of affected people", and the Durban Action Plan specifies the key targets to be achieved, including poverty alleviation[54], participatory management settings[55] and improved governance.[56]

Good governance principles

"Governance of protected areas" is a relatively new concept[57] in the conservation field and it first rose to prominence at the Durban Congress. Governance is about power, relationships, responsibility and accountability.[58] Some define it as "the interactions among structures, processes and traditions that determine how power is exercised, how decisions are taken on issues of public concern, and how citizens or other stakeholders have their say".[59] Thus it is the combination of explicit and implicit policies, practices and institutions that affect public life. In a protected area context, governance covers a broad range of issues – from policy to practice, from behaviour to meaning, from investments to impacts. It is crucially related to the achievement of protected area objectives (management effectiveness), determines the sharing of relevant costs and benefits (management equity), is key to preventing or solving social conflicts, and affects the generation and sustenance of public support.

---

[53] In particular in element 2 of the work programme for protected areas.

[54] See also Recommendation 5.29 of the 5th World Parks Congress, 2003.

[55] See also Recommendation 5.24 and 525 produced at the 5th World Parks Congress, 2003.

[56] See also Recommendations 5.16 and 5.17 produced at the 5th World Parks Congress, 2003.

[57] See Graham *et al.*, 2003; Abrams *et al.*, 2003; Jaireth and Smyth, 2003; Borrini-Feyerabend, 2003; Borrini-Feyerabend, 2004; CBD, 2004.

[58] UNDP, 1999; UNDP, 2002.

[59] Graham *et al.*, 2003.

The Durban Congress developed a set of "good governance" principles for protected areas, including:

- *"legitimacy and voice"* – ensuring the capacity of men and women to influence decisions, on the basis of freedom of association and speech;

- *"subsidiarity"* – attributing management authority and responsibility to the institutions closest to the resources at stake; [60]

- *"fairness"* – sharing equitably the costs and benefits of conservation and providing a recourse to impartial judgement in case of conflict;

- *"do no harm!"* – making sure that the costs of conservation are not "dumped" on some weak social actors without any form of compensation;

- *"direction"* – establishing long-term conservation objectives grounded in an appreciation of ecological, historical, social and cultural complexities;

- *"performance"* – meeting the needs and concerns of all stakeholders while making a wise use of resources; and

- *"accountability"* – having clearly demarcated lines of responsibility and ensuring a transparent flow of information about processes and institutions.

The above principles are very important but overarching them is the most basic criterion for "good governance", namely the respect for human rights. A *"rights-based approach"* is thus considered by many as the most equitable path to conservation (as noted, this is now an established part of the IUCN view of conservation). The rights-based approach to conservation advocated at Durban and the good governance principles in general "represent an ideal that no society has fully attained or realized",[61] but many of them are being pursued in protected area contexts, providing on-going experiences and learning. In this respect, another innovative perspective that rose to prominence at the Durban Congress regards the recognition of the unique rights of *mobile* indigenous peoples (see Box 2.1).

New "governance types" for protected areas

Neither the CBD nor the IUCN definitions limit "protected areas" to those territories and resources owned, designated and/or managed by national or regional/provincial government authorities, and several countries have adopted legislation that accurately reflects this broad concept of protected area. Furthermore, the 1992 World Parks Congress in Caracas (Venezuela) fully recognised that various types of landowners (communal, individual or corporate) can play a crucial role in conservation, and this was in turn reflected in the guidelines on the IUCN protected area categories.[62] Despite this, many still assume that to qualify as a 'protected area', the land or water must be set up, owned and managed by a branch of government.

---

[60] This latter tenet derives from a number of religious and cultural traditions and is now enshrined in European Community Law.

[61] Graham *et al.*, 2003.

[62] IUCN, 1994.

The idea of setting a territory or sea area under a special regime – from total seclusion and protection to controlled and regulated use – has a long history and has been widely adopted. Thus, for thousands of years, indigenous and local communities, kings and other rulers, aristocrats, priests and shamans have set up what we would now call conservation regimes, with rules regulating or forbidding access to natural resources.

In contrast, the history of official protected areas is much more recent.[63] As a matter of fact, many formally designated protected areas overlapped with, and incorporated, preexisting areas conserved by indigenous peoples and local and mobile communities (see

---

Box 2.1   Mobile Indigenous Peoples at the Vth World Parks Congress, Durban, 2003

An unprecedented number of mobile[64] indigenous peoples participated in the Vth World Parks Congress in Durban (September 2003) and were able to articulate the case for their contribution to conservation. It was the first time such a group had come together in an international protected areas forum. Mobile indigenous peoples defined themselves as "a subset of traditional and indigenous peoples whose livelihoods depend on extensive common property use of natural resources and whose mobility is both a management strategy for sustainable land use and conservation and a distinctive source of cultural identity".[65]

The history of protected areas includes many examples of alienation of these peoples from the lands and resources they have traditionally used, with consequent loss of livelihoods and erosion of their cultures. Their rights have very often been ignored. Indeed, mobile people have frequently been excluded from even from those limited opportunities provided to sedentary indigenous people, for instance some "consultation" on land management options. Yet, the practices of mobile indigenous peoples create and sustain important linkages in the landscape through bio-cultural corridors,[66] which promote environmental integrity and the conservation of both wild and domesticated biodiversity.

Recommendation 5.27 of the Durban Congress highlighted the cultural landscapes shaped by mobile people and recognised that such groups can be powerful partners for conservation. Affirming the importance of their traditional and evolving institutions and norms, it argued that the mobile indigenous peoples' rights to co-manage or self-manage their lands should be secured, that they should derive equitable benefits from the use of natural resources, that their traditional cross-border mobility and trade in transboundary protected areas should be maintained, and that their traditional knowledge, institutions, customary laws and resource management practices should be respected and integrated into protected area management. It highlighted that mobile indigenous peoples have the right to demand the restitution of the lands, territories and resources that they have traditionally conserved, occupied and sustainably used and that were subsequently incorporated into protected areas without their consent. It affirmed their right to restore their mobile livelihoods, if those have been impeded.

---

[63]   It is usually dated from the establishment of the Yellowstone National Park in Wyoming, USA in 1872, or the even earlier establishment of Yosemite National Park (Colchester, 2003).

[64]   The term "mobile peoples" was adopted at the Dana Conference of 2002 as the most useful term to describe peoples commonly referred to as "nomadic." The term "mobile" was considered more inclusive, as it applies to hunters and gatherers, "sea gypsies", shifting cultivators and other groups that have an attachment to particular landscapes and seascapes rather than to definite places only.

[65]   See Dana Declaration, 2002 (at: www.danadeclaration.org/). In sharp contrast with "open access" regimes, common property systems have well-established community rules for use/ownership and often encompass Community Conserved Areas.

[66]   Presentation by T. Farvar and S. Soltani at the Global Biodiversity Forum of Kuala Lumpur, February 2004.

Chapter 4) and/or private reserves. Indeed it is likely that most government-run protected areas in the world have been created in areas traditionally inhabited or used by indigenous and local communities. Often, the communities had in place their own conservation practices, including some quite elaborate and effective systems, which were "replaced" by official regulations based on state ownership of natural resources. In other cases, such conservation practices still exist, inside or outside the protected areas.

While there is little reliable information about the full extent of territories and resources protected by indigenous and local communities and private landowners, either today or in historical times,[67] it has been estimated that between 400 to 800 million hectares of forest is currently owned or administered by communities.[68] A large part of the world's biodiversity, moreover, remains outside government-established protected areas, in forests, rangelands, mountain environments, wetlands, freshwater bodies and coastal and marine environments (including mangroves, coral reefs and sea grass beds) within land or on water that is state-owned, under private property, or held in communal ownership. Many of the involved indigenous and local communities apply a variety of management regimes for these resources that range from an outright emphasis on resource use to an emphasis on respect and preservation guided by spiritual, cultural or aesthetic objectives. Among the latter are strictly protected elements, such as sacred groves or areas with limited and codified access and use. In fact, a variety of community management efforts, be they strict protection or use-oriented, are *effective* in conserving biodiversity and the associated ecological service and cultural values and, as described in Chapter 5, they can be considered examples of "Community Conserved Areas".

Are these Community Conserved Areas 'protected areas' as defined by IUCN and CBD? A commonsense interpretation of these definitions suggests that for a place to be recognised as a protected area, it should meet these tests:

- be an area-based instrument;

- involve an explicit and declared intent to protect and maintain biodiversity (e.g. through dedication or designation) that *may* also be recognised by government, and/or involve explicit measures (e.g. regulation) for the purposes of biodiversity conservation;

- be managed through legal or other effective means (including customary law);

- have some kind of management body in place (including community-based institutions); and

- be intended to continue indefinitely into the future.

On the basis of the available evidence, it would appear that most Community Conserved Areas meet the above tests and can therefore be considered to be protected areas.

The practical significance of this in relation to national systems of protected areas is discussed further in Chapter 5. However, if the contribution of Community Conserved Areas to biodiversity is officially recognised,[69] it would become possible to see the

---

[67]   MacDonald, 2003.

[68]   Molnar *et al.*, 2003.

landscape/seascape as a mosaic of areas and resource units under different ownerships, uses and regulations, possibly including several government-run protected areas, along with Community Conserved Areas, Co-managed Protected Areas and even private reserves (owned or managed for example by individuals, conservation NGOs, corporations and universities). The possibility of dealing with a whole spectrum of conservation initiatives is important for conservation, as localised results can be linked, harmonised and combined, and can, overall, enrich one another in synergistic ways.

In the light of the above, governmental agencies, communities and private landowners are all actual or potential key actors in conservation. While the role of governments is well understood (at least at the national and provincial levels), that of indigenous and local communities[70], and the contribution of the private sector have been generally less appreciated. This is why the reflection carried out at the Durban Congress on "governance type" is so important.

"Governance", in this context, relates to IUCN's understanding of a protected area, or the understanding developed by the CBD Conference of Parties (see above). A basic distinction between governance types can be made on the basis of "who holds management authority and responsibility and can be held accountable according to legal, customary or otherwise legitimate rights".[71] Accordingly, four main protected area governance "types" were identified and discussed[72] at the Durban Congress:

A. Government managed protected areas

B. Co-managed Protected Areas

C. Private protected areas

D. Community Conserved Areas

These are briefly described in Box 2.2 below.

This understanding of governance types is relevant to the pursuit of equity in conservation. Community Conserved Areas or Co-managed Protected Areas can only be understood within a particular historical and social context, often as indicators of institutional continuity, strength or change. Modernization processes occurring throughout the world have undermined indigenous, mobile and local communities and devalued the roles they play in natural resource management. Their "re-discovery" at the Durban Parks Congress[73] – while acknowledging the many constraints and pitfalls that apply to community-based conservation – is relevant to equity as it raises the question: "is the governance type in place for a given protected area *fair* in the light of historical conditions, customary and legal rights and impact on the relevant communities?"

As demonstrated by the case examples presented at the Congress and described in the literature,[74] many conflicts between protected areas and communities could be avoided

---

[69] In which case it should be done, as illustrated in Chapter 5, without prejudice to the community institutions that established and managed it.

[70] See Article 8(j) of the Convention on Biological Diversity.

[71] Borrini-Feyerabend, 2004.

[72] See Recommendations no. 5.17; 5.25; 5.26 and 5.27 of the 5th World Parks Congress, 2003.

[73] See Recommendation 5.26 on Community Conserved Areas.

Box 2.2 Governance types for protected areas

A: Government Managed Protected Areas.

Most people are familiar with type A governance, in which a government body (such as a Ministry or Park Agency reporting directly to the government) holds the authority, responsibility and accountability for managing the protected area, determines its conservation objectives (such as the ones that distinguish the IUCN categories), subjects it to a management regime, and often also owns the protected area's land, water and related resources. Reflecting the trend towards greater devolution in general in many countries, sub-national and municipal government bodies have recently also become prominent in declaring and managing protected areas. In some cases, the state retains full land ownership and/or control or oversight of protected areas but delegates their management to a para-statal organization, NGO or even a private operator or community. The government may or may not have a legal obligation to inform or consult other identified stakeholders prior to setting up protected areas and making or enforcing management decisions.

B: Co-managed Protected Areas.

Type B governance, which is developed further in Chapter 4 of these Guidelines, is also becoming increasingly common, responding to the variety of interlocked entitlements recognised by democratic societies. Complex processes and institutional mechanisms are generally employed to share management authority and responsibility among a plurality of actors – from national to sub-national (including local) government authorities, from representatives of indigenous, mobile and local communities to user associations, private entrepreneurs and land-owners. The actors recognise the legitimacy of their respective entitlements to manage the protected area and agree on subjecting it to a specific conservation objective (such as the ones that distinguish the IUCN categories). Distinct co-management sub-types may be identified. In collaborative management, for instance, formal decision-making authority, responsibility and accountability may rest with one agency (often a national governmental agency), but the agency is required – by law or policy – to collaborate with other stakeholders. In its weak form, "collaboration" means informing and consulting stakeholders. In its strong form, "collaboration" means that a multi-stakeholder body develops and approves by consensus a number of technical proposals for protected area regulation and management, to be later submitted to the decision-making authority. In joint management, various actors sit on a management body with decision-making authority, responsibility and accountability. Again, the requirements for joint management are made stronger if decision-making is carried out by consensus. When this is not the case, the balance of power reflected in the composition of the joint manaent body may *de facto* transform it into a different governance type (e.g. when government actors or private landowners hold an absolute majority of votes). Because of the many actors which are often involved, some form of multi-stakeholder management may be particularly suited to the needs of many transboundary protected areas.[75]

C: Private Protected Areas.

Type C governance has a relatively long history, as kings and aristocracies often preserved for themselves certain areas of land or the privilege to hunt wildlife. Such private reserves had important secondary conservation benefits. Today, private ownership is still an enormously important force in conservation. Private reserves include areas under individual, cooperative, corporate for-profit, and corporate not-for-profit ownership. Conservation NGOs buy areas of land, which in some cases are large, and dedicate them to conservation. Many individual landowners pursue conservation objectives out of respect for the land or a desire to maintain its beauty and ecological value. Utilitarian purposes, such as gaining

---

[74] See www.iucn.org/themes/ceesp/Wkg_grp/TILCEPA/community.htm; IUCN/CEESP, 2002; IUCN/CEESP, 2003; Brechin *et al.*, 2003.

[75] Sandwith *et al.*, 2001.

Box 2.2   Governance types for protected areas (cont.)

revenue from ecotourism or reducing levies and taxes, are additional incentives. In all these cases, authority for managing the protected land and resources rests with the landowners, who determine a conservation objective, impose a conservation regime and are responsible for decision-making, subject to applicable legislation and usually under terms agreed with the respective governments. Their accountability to the larger society, however, is usually quite limited. Some forms of accountability may be negotiated with the government in exchange for specific incentives (as in the case of Easements or Land Trusts).

D: Community Conserved Areas.

This governance type involves governance by indigenous, mobile and local communities. This may be the oldest form of protected area governance and it is still widespread (see a number of examples in Chapter 5). Throughout the world and over thousands of years, human communities have shaped their lifestyles and livelihood strategies to respond to the opportunities and challenges presented by their surrounding land and natural resources. In so doing, they simultaneously manage, modify and often conserve and enrich their environments. In many cases, community interaction with the environment generated a sort of symbiosis, which some refer to as "bio-cultural units" or "cultural landscapes/seascapes". Much of this interaction happened not for the intentional conservation of biodiversity but in pursuit of a variety of interlocked objectives and values (spiritual, religious, security-related, survival-related), which did, however, result in the conservation of ecosystems, species and ecosystem-related services. In this sense, Community Conserved Areas comprise "natural and modified ecosystems including significant biodiversity, ecological services and cultural values voluntarily conserved by indigenous, mobile and local communities through customary laws or other effective means". In Community Conserved Areas, authority and responsibility rest with the communities through a variety of forms of ethnic governance or locally agreed organizations and rules. These forms and rules are very diverse and can be extremely complex. For instance, land and/or some resources may be collectively owned and managed, but other resources may be individually owned and managed or managed on a clan-basis.[76] Nearly every community has developed management regulations and organizations, which may or may not be legally sanctioned at the national level.

In Community Conserved Areas, the community's accountability to the larger society remains usually limited, although it may be defined as part of broader negotiations with the national government and other partners, possibly as a counterpart to being assured, for example, the recognition of collective land rights, the respect for customary practices and the provision of economic incentives. Such negotiations may even result in a joint management arrangement among indigenous and local communities, government actors and other stakeholders (thus changing the governance type from D to B). Some communities organize themselves in various ways, including legal forms such as NGOs, to manage their resources. This may not change the governance type from D to C, if the NGO remains accountable to the authority of the respective community.

---

and replaced by constructive cooperation if communities were recognised as rightful managers or co-managers of the natural resources on which they depend for their livelihoods and cultural identity. In other words, effective and meaningful participation of relevant communities in the governance of the land and resources to be conserved is vital to conservation success. In this sense both Community Conserved Areas and Co-managed Protected Areas encourage greater equity because they allow the effective

---

[76]   An instructive example can be found in Baird and Dearden, 2003.

engagement of communities in conservation while attempting to meet basic human needs, and respecting human rights.[77]

Governance types and the IUCN Protected Areas Management Categories

This new understanding of governance types for protected areas can be related to the IUCN category classification. Two points of principle should be noted:

- only areas that meet the IUCN definition of a protected area are included in this analysis,

- but any area that can be considered as protected area should be capable of being assigned *both* to a protected area management category *and* to a governance type.

These principles are applied in Table 2.1, where governance type is illustrated as a complementary dimension to the IUCN category system. This indicates that governance types are *category-neutral* and that protected areas exist that fill each possible combination of management category and governance type. This model has been discussed in the literature and at the Durban Congress and is increasingly recognised as generally applicable. Even for the most strictly protected area categories, such as category Ia (strict nature reserve), all four governance types occur. For example, some of the most valuable wilderness areas in the world correspond to territories under the control of un-contacted peoples, in the Amazon and some other forests in the Tropics – communities which have conserved their environments as part of an unbending resistance to contacts of any kind from outside.[78] This volume deals mostly, if not exclusively, with Categories B (Co-managed Protected Areas) and D (Community Conserved Areas).

The CBD targets

The Durban message to the CBD recommended that the Conference of Parties ensure full participation of indigenous peoples and local communities in the establishment and management of protected areas. It called for policy reform to facilitate Community Conserved Areas and co-management, together with a strengthened poverty focus and integration of the Millennium Development Goals into protected area performance criteria. It re-emphasised that the IUCN protected area management categories were to be used as a framework for planning, managing and monitoring protected areas, while calling for new guidance to implement them, in particular regarding cultural and spiritual values and the role of local and indigenous communities as managers.

---

[77] See Recommendation 5.25 on Co-managed Protected Areas and, before that, the WCC Resolutions 1.42 (Montreal, 1996) and 2.15 (Amman, 2000).

[78] For a more detailed analysis of how the IUCN categories relate to Community Conserved Areas, see Table 5.1 in Chapter 5.

Table 2.1   A classification system for protected areas comprising both management category and governance type

Governance types / PA Categories	A. Government Managed Protected Areas			B. Co-managed Protected Areas			C. Private Protected Areas			D. Community Conserved Areas	
	Federal or national ministry or agency in charge	Local/ municipal ministry or agency in change	Government-delegated management (e.g. to an NGO)	Transboundary management	Collaborative management (various forms of pluralist influence)	Joint management (pluralist management board)	Declared and run by individual land-owner	... by non-profit organizations (e.g. NGOs, universities, co-operatives)	... by for profit organizations (e.g. individual or corporate land-owners)	Declared and run by indigenous peoples	Declared and run by local communities
Ia – Strict Nature Reserve											
Ib – Wilderness Area											
II – National Park											
III – Natural Monument											
IV – Habitat/ Species Management											
V – Protected Landscape/ Seascape											
VI – Managed Resource Protected Area											

The CBD/COP7 responded very positively to the call, including in its Programme of Work on Protected Areas Element 2 on "Governance, Equity, Participation and Benefit Sharing", which calls on the Parties to the Convention to achieve measurable targets by 2012 or earlier.[79] The key concepts of governance, equity, participation and benefit sharing are not exclusively dealt with in Element 2, but are embedded in all the elements of the work programme.

Regarding *governance*, the CBD programme of work asks for the development of better practices and stronger patterns of accountability. It urges Parties to recognise and promote various protected area governance types in national and regional systems and to support Community Conserved Areas through particular policies and legal, financial and community means. Regarding *equity,* the programme of work establishes that prior informed consent is required before any indigenous community is relocated for the establishment of a protected area. Regarding *participation,* the programme of work asks for participatory planning and the involvement of all relevant stakeholders. It stresses the appreciation of local knowledge and sustainable uses of natural resources, and the need to better understand the needs, priorities, practices and values of indigenous and

---

[79]   For the full text of this programme, see www.biodiv.org/decisions/default.aspx?m=COP-07&id=7765&lg=0.

local communities. To this end, it calls for studies, constructive dialogue, exchanges of information and experiences, and joint research among local and non-local experts. Regarding *benefit sharing,* the programme of work calls for a more equitable division of the costs and benefits of conservation, in particular for indigenous and local communities. It also asks Parties to make use of conservation benefits to reduce poverty.

Specifically, among the targets to be reached and reported upon by the Parties to the CBD in the coming years are the following (*emphasis added*):

- Target 1.4: All protected areas to have effective management in existence by 2012, using *participatory* and science-based site planning processes that incorporate clear biodiversity objectives, targets, management strategies and monitoring programmes, drawing upon existing methodologies and a long-term management plan *with active stakeholder involvement.*

- Target 2.1: Establish by 2008 mechanisms for the *equitable sharing of both costs and benefits* arising from the establishment and management of protected areas.

- Target 2.2: *Full and effective participation* by 2008, *of indigenous and local communities,* in *full respect of their rights and recognition of their responsibilities,* consistent with national law and applicable international obligations, and *the participation of relevant stakeholders* in the management of existing, and the establishment and management of new, protected areas.

- Target 4.1: By 2008, *standards, criteria, and best practices for* planning, selecting, establishing, managing and *governance* of national and regional systems of protected areas are developed and adopted.

These targets are sufficient to open new horizons and assign new tasks for professionals and activists engaged in conservation policy and practice in the next decade. The programme of work calls for a positive response by all Parties to the CBD, which should begin with taking stock of their current situation and opportunities for action.

3. Taking stock of your situation

Conservationists face a sensitive task. They need to identify areas and resources of remarkable biodiversity and promote their conservation in every possible way. In most cases this has meant assisting national and local governments to establish protected areas— an option embraced by virtually all countries of the world, which so far managed to achieve some form of protection over nearly 12% of the earth's land surface. But this magnificent achievement, which was properly celebrated at the Vth World Parks Congress of 2003, is not yet enough. There are two immense tasks waiting to be tackled. First, all existing protected areas need to be well managed, often much *better* managed than they are today, requiring enhanced attention, resources, solutions to outstanding conflicts and, at times, altogether different management approaches. Secondly, much valuable biodiversity exists *outside* government-established protected areas and it too needs to be conserved as far as possible. A partial solution to both challenges lies in the analyses provided in Chapters 1 and 2: through better engagement with local and indigenous communities, the prospects for conservation in many protected areas can be improved; and the "conservation estate" can be expanded by incorporating effective and innovative conservation options in addition to official protected areas. These Guidelines have been designed with such opportunities in mind, and specifically to assist professionals willing to respond to Element 2 of the CBD Programme of Work on Protected Areas – on Governance, Participation, Equity and Benefit Sharing – and to pursue the related targets discussed in Chapter 2.

The starting point is to take stock of the specific situation facing each user, or team of users, of this volume. This requires that they are familiar not only with governance Types A, B and C (Box 2.2) but also take account of Community Conserved Areas (Type D). Table 3.1 and Figure 3.1 offer questions and considerations designed to help to identify key concerns with regard to communities, equity and protected areas. Thereafter, the reader will be directed towards the chapters and sections of this volume that are most relevant for their situation.

A significant question about a government-established protected area governing body is whether it embraces an "exclusive" or "inclusive" approach with respect to local stakeholders,[80] in particular to indigenous peoples and local and mobile communities. The exclusive approach has a tradition rooted in the early protected area practice in the USA and other countries, and asserts the primacy of "common values" and the "common good" at the level of a country, or state, over the particular values and interests of local people.[81] It typically includes protected areas dedicated to the protection of wilderness and ecosystem functions, and it effectively de-couples the interests of local people from the areas concerned. This approach has often involved the removal and resettlement of resident communities outside the park area. By contrast, the inclusive approach sees the interests of local societies as central to the protected area ("the well-being of those who live and work in the National Parks must always be a first consideration ... "[82]), is

---

[80]   West and Brechin, 1991.

[81]   The local communities may also seek the "common good" but they are likely to define this by reference to their own ethical, cultural, or economic interests.

Box 3.1   What are your key concerns with regard to communities, equity and protected areas?

- Do you mostly deal with conservation policy? Is your area of reference broad (regional, national, or international), encompassing one or more systems of protected areas?

- Do you principally, or to a considerable extent, deal with conservation at a landscape/ seascape level, possibly concerning one or more official protected areas and/or Community Conserved Areas (CCAs)?

- If you are principally concerned with official protected areas, are those managed with or without the effective involvement of the relevant indigenous and local communities?

- If you are principally concerned with areas managed and conserved by indigenous and local communities, are those recognised by the relevant governmental agencies at various levels?

- Are there any open conflicts regarding the management decisions relating to official protected areas or CCAs? Are those minor or serious? From whose point of view?

- Are there un-tapped opportunities for collaboration regarding official protected areas and CCAs? On the basis of what (what are the "reasons for hope")?

- For each relevant site, fundamental insights usually come from history. When was each official protected area and/or CCA established? For what purposes?[83]

- Have the relevant indigenous and local communities recognised and accepted the establishment of the relevant official protected areas? Have they ever acted violently or violated protected area regulations? Conversely, was there any violent imposition over their will and traditional practices?

- Have governmental agencies recognised and acknowledged the community management of CCAs? Have they ever supported it? Have they violated its basic tenets and rules?

- What vision inspires and informs the official protected area or CCA managers? Does that vision include a place for other social actors? Does it reflect the historical, cultural and social complexities of the context at stake? Does it recognise a plurality of ways to understand and value nature and protect biodiversity, and a plurality of "grounds" (entitlements) on which various parties can ask to be involved in management?

- Are there mechanisms that enable local/traditional and mainstream knowledge and practices to be integrated and used in a complementary and respectful way? For an official protected area, are there mechanisms by which the indigenous peoples and local and mobile communities are involved in planning, taking decisions, implementing plans, sharing the benefits of conservation, monitoring and evaluating the management result? For a CCA, are there contacts between local managers and other social actors, including government agencies? Are specific agreements ever developed? Is the management setting of the protected area or CCA described by anyone as "co-management"?

- Are human rights respected in matters relevant to the official protected area or CCA?

- Are controversies being dealt with impartially and through the rule of formal and/or customary law?

---

[82]   Harmon, 1991.

[83]   At times one has to investigate rather deeply to identify the real reasons for the establishment of a protected area or a Community Conserved Area. For government-managed protected areas, for instance, the real reasons may not coincide with official statements and the objectives stated in the management plan. For Community Conserved Areas, the real reasons may have been forgotten and the practice may have remained as part of local customs.

Box 3.1   What are your key concerns with regard to communities, equity and protected areas? (cont.)

- Are decisions being taken at the lowest level where capacity is available?

- Are there mechanisms to assure transparency and accountability in decision-making regarding the official protected area or CCA?

- Are decision makers responsive to the concerns of various concerned parties? Do they value their contributions? Do they seek social consensus?

- Are there pluralist governance structures in place, devoted to dialogue and developing negotiated agreements? Are there any other mechanisms to allow the involvement of the relevant parties in the management of the official protected area or CCA?

- Who enjoys (most of) the benefits of conservation? Who bears (most of) the costs? Are there mechanisms that assess and ensure an equitable sharing of the benefits and costs of conservation? Are those effective?

- What are the biodiversity and other conservation outcomes of the conservation initiative? Is it clear what is needed to achieve conservation? It is clear where the key problems and opportunities lie?

- Is the legal and policy environment supportive? Are the necessary technical capacities in place?

- On the basis of your answers to the above questions, what are the key issues and threats standing in the way of enhanced conservation and equity in your context of concern?

entirely compatible with community or private ownership of land within protected areas and seeks the involvement of local administrators in management planning. Such an approach can be identified in Category V protected areas (Protected Landscapes/ Seascapes) in many countries in Europe (see Box 3.2).

Box 3.2   A "typical" European protected area? A co-managed landscape
(adapted from Statham, 1994)

Is there such a thing as a typical protected area in Europe? Possibly not, but if one existed it would not be too different from the North York Moors National Park, a Category V protected area in the United Kingdom that includes land that is settled and has been farmed for millennia. The landscape encompasses large areas of semi-natural vegetation, such as ancient woodlands, interspersed with grazing areas, hedgerows, farmland, and some small towns and villages. The relationship between the park and the local people is so close that the Park Management Plan is included as part of the general plan of Town and Country Development, prepared with the extensive involvement of the public. In fact, the majority of the North York Moors is under private ownership (a factor common to many other protected areas in Europe) and the management plan is therefore dependent on the co-operation of the landowners. While building and engineering works are controlled in part by the Park Authority (normally without compensation), farming and land management activities generally remain outside their control. To ensure that farming and land management activities conform to the park plan, agreements are often signed between the landowners and the Park Authority. Though considered to be legally binding contracts, these agreements are entirely voluntary, although the Park Authority provides financial incentives and compensation in return for agreed works or management practices.

Consideration of whether an exclusive or inclusive approach is preferable is best undertaken in the light of particular ecological and socio-economic contexts. An exclusive model that helps conserve wilderness and scenic beauty in a largely uninhabited land should not be applied without regard for the potential adverse consequences in territories traditionally inhabited by people who depend on the local resources for their livelihood and cultural identity. Yet, it is the exclusive approach that has been commonly applied in many countries, where community livelihoods very often depend directly on natural resources. More inclusive management partnerships have come to the fore only recently, often through a slow process of "disentangling" protected areas from the "guns and fences" and/or the paternalistic or authoritarian attitudes of the past.[84]

In reality, protected area governance is more complex than any simple dual model (e.g., inclusive/exclusive) can describe. A continuum of options exists for sharing authority between the governmental agency "in charge" (referred to as the "protected area agency", for short) and the concerned communities (see Figure 3.1).

Figure 3.1   Protected area agencies and communities – a continuum of governance options[85]

Along the continuum of Figure 3.1, and according to what they consider possible and desirable in legal, political, financial and social terms, government protected area agencies may:

- **ignore** the interests and capacities of indigenous peoples and local and mobile communities, and **repress** all unlawful relationships with the protected area (the pure exclusive model); or

- **inform** them about relevant issues and decisions;

- actively **consult** them about such issues and decisions;

- **seek their consensus** on issues and decisions, also through sharing with them some economic and other benefits of conservation;

---

[84]   Borrini-Feyerabend and Sandwith, 2003.

[85]   Adapted from Borrini-Feyerabend, 1996.

- **negotiate** with them on an open basis (thus effectively involving them in the decision-making process) and develop specific co-management agreements;

- **share** with them **authority** and **responsibilities** in a formal way (e.g., by asking them to join a Management Board), thus creating a co-management organization; or

- **recognise** their existing **management authority and responsibility** or **restitute/ devolve** such authority and responsibility to them (e.g. as a consequence of a legal claim, restitution process or reform in the country's protected area system).

Similar graduated options could also be identified from the perspective of indigenous and local communities with regard to outside interference with Community Conserved Areas. Communities may be more or less keen to involve the governmental agencies and other parties in decision-making regarding the territories and natural resources of their concern.

On the basis of the questions listed in Box 3.1 and the schematic representation in Figure 3.1, it should be possible to identify which parts of these Guidelines are most relevant to the reader (see Table 3.1).

Table 3.1   How to use this volume to respond to your key concerns

Your situation/concerns	Chapters most relevant for you
Dealing with international, national or regional conservation policy, and/or with systems and networks of protected areas (including Community Conserved Areas (CCAs))	Chapter 6, but parts of Chapters 4 and 5 would also be useful.
Dealing with landscape or seascape conservation, encompassing one or more official protected area and/or CCAs	Some of the policy options in Chapter 6, but also Chapters 4 or 5 (depending on whether you deal with official protected areas and/or CCA s or both).
Dealing with a particular government-managed protected area	Chapter 4 and, possibly, also Chapter 6. But you should be informed also about the innovative options described in Chapter 5.
Dealing with a specific protected area under a co-management regime	As above.
Dealing with a specific CCA	Chapter 5 and Chapter 6 to identify possible activities for policy support.
Dealing with landscapes or seascapes that could eventually include new official protected areas or CCAs	Chapter 6 plus some of the options listed in Chapters 4 and 5.
Dealing with management conflicts between governmental agencies and communities	Chapter 4 or 5 depending on whether the conflict involves a government managed or Co-managed Protected Area (Ch. 4) or a CCA (Ch. 5). Some policy options described in Chapter 6 may also be relevant.
Dealing with scarce local participation in the management of official protected areas, and poor compliance with rules	Chapter 4 and some of the policy options in Chapter 6.
Dealing with problems of management effectiveness in official protected areas and/or CCAs	Chapters 4 or 5, as relevant, and some of the policy options in Chapter 6.
Dealing with problems of poverty and unsustainable livelihoods affecting, or being affected by official protected areas and CCAs	Chapter 6, but also Chapters 4 and 5, if poverty and unsustainable livelihoods are closely related to an official protected area or CCA
Dealing with problems of violated human rights and unrecognised customary laws and practices in official protected areas and CCAs	Chapters 4 or 5, as relevant. And several policy options in Chapter 6

4. Guidelines for Co-managed Protected Areas

Most government-designated and managed protected areas are governed by decision-making bodies created within governmental or semi-governmental institutions in accordance with national and/or regional legislation and policies. These bodies include national protected area agencies, ministerial departments, *ad-hoc* authorities, para-statal institutions, municipal or provincial governments or multi-party bodies of legally-determined composition—encompassing a broad variety of types and approaches. In some cases, governments have delegated responsibility for aspects of protected areas work to NGOs. Some of these bodies have ample autonomy, a large work-force and an impressive budget.

At times the governmental agency at national, sub-national or local level that officially declared the area under a protected status collaborates with other parties to develop and implement management plans and associated agreements. If the collaboration is significant, the protected area is said to be under a collaborative, joint, multi-stakeholder or co-management regime, or, in short to be a *Co-managed Protected Area.* We thus define[86] Co-managed Protected Areas as:

> "*government-designated protected areas where decision making power, responsibility and accountability are shared between governmental agencies and other stakeholders, in particular the indigenous peoples and local and mobile communities that depend on that area culturally and/or for their livelihoods*".

A co-management governance type is thus in place when a number of parties – including the governmental agency at national, sub-national or local level that has officially declared the area under a protected status – engage in some form of negotiation around a management plan. The management plan is generally part of a broader agreement, including complementary initiatives, by-laws, incentives and compensations.[87] The latter are negotiated together with the plan ("package agreement") and often make all the difference for some of the negotiating actors. Besides the agreement (co-management plan and complementary measures), the process usually ends up establishing one or more multi-party management organizations, with mandates for advice, development of technical proposals, or outright decision-making.

Who are the "legitimate" parties that should negotiate a co-management regime? This question can only be answered with reference to a specific context (and, even for a specific context, the answer may change through time). Of key relevance here is that the

---

[86] This definition developed through the 1990s building upon, among others, the work of West and Brechin, 1991; Berkes, George and Preston, 1991; Borrini-Feyerabend, 1996; Kothari *et al.*, 1996; IUCN, 1996; Renard, 1997; Stevens, 1997; 1998; NRTEE, 1998. The term is now of common use for protected areas as well as for natural resources in general. See Borrini-Feyerabend *et al.*, 2004, [in press].

[87] Guidance on the content of a management plan can be found in Thomas and Middleton, 2003.

indigenous and local communities who have traditionally owned, occupied or used lands and resources within protected areas can claim customary and/or legal rights to lands and resources based on ancient possession, continuity of relationship, historical ties, cultural ties and direct dependency on the resources. At the minimum they can be considered primary stakeholders, and at times are holders of primary rights under national legislation. If communities have stronger claims and entitlements vis-à-vis recent and opportunistic resource users, several other actors can be co-management partners, including semi-governmental bodies, NGOs, private operators (e.g. those providing tourist facilities) and businesses and corporations. Different actors, however, have different stakes and entitlements with respect to the protected area, and co-management arrangements need *not* give them equal weight in consultation and decision-making. Box 4.1 lists several criteria that can help distinguish between primary and other stakeholders.

Box 4.1 Possible criteria to distinguish among primary and other stakeholders in protected areas
(adapted from Borrini-Feyerabend, 1996)

- existing legal or customary rights to the land or natural resources included in the protected area;

- continuity of relationship with such land and resources (e.g. residents versus visitors and tourists);

- direct dependency on the natural resources in question for subsistence and survival (e.g. for food, water, medicine, housing);

- historical and cultural relations with the land and resources;

- unique knowledge, skills and institutions for the management of the resources;

- degree of economic and social reliance (dependence) on such resources;

- losses and damage incurred in the management process (e.g. related to human-wildlife conflicts);

- degree of demonstrated effort and interest in management;

- compatibility of the interests and activities of the stakeholder with national conservation and development policies;

- compatibility of the interests and activities of the stakeholder with international conventions and agreements subscribed to by the country concerned.

The process by which a protected area acquires co-management status may be smooth or arise out of controversy and conflict. In several countries, co-management is enshrined in the legislation that establishes and regulates protected areas: the legislation prescribes that co-management boards have to be multi-party bodies. In some cases it also identifies which "parties" need to be represented,[88] and in others the parties are identified through rather complex and lengthy processes of social discussion.[89] However, other

---

[88] An example is Italy's Law 349, which prescribes that protected area management boards should have 12 members, including a national representative of the Ministry of the Environment, a regional representative of the same Ministry, up to four mayors of the local involved municipalities, a representative of the regional university, up to two representatives of conservation NGOs, etc.

[89] An example is the Regional Nature Parks system of France, in which both local elected administrators and the local organized civil society develop together a "Charter" outlining the objectives and rules of each individual protected area (Allali-Puz *et al.*, 2003).

countries' protected area laws foresee that management is to be carried out exclusively by a governmental agency. In such cases, other interested parties, including indigenous peoples and local and mobile communities, will need to "gain" access to management through political means of all kinds, or through pilot demonstration projects and the like.

The mechanisms for engagement of stakeholders will vary greatly according to the context, but are likely to include becoming members of an advisory or decision-making body. In the latter case, there is an important distinction between deciding by majority voting or by consensus. The critical factors with majority voting are the number of votes assigned to each party and the alliances likely to be created among them. In the case of consensus, the institutional arrangements can be more sophisticated (see Box 4.2) and actually embed process incentives in favour of decisions that are both equitable and sustainable.

Box 4.2   Consensus in a co-management board: a key incentive towards effective and equitable management of the Galapagos Marine Reserve
(adapted from Heylings and Bravo, 2001)

Located approximately 1,000km from the Ecuadorian mainland, the volcanic Galapagos Islands contain remarkable terrestrial and marine ecosystems and became, some years ago, the focus of complex and sometimes violent multi-stakeholder conflicts. The rapid economic and demographic change, the presence of unregulated industrial fishing, the appearance of high-value fisheries for Asian markets, the state-imposed policy and regulations and the general non-compliance with the management plan of the Marine Reserve were all factors fuelling those conflicts. In 1998, in response to national and international concern about the threats facing them, Ecuador passed innovative legislation through a Special Law that, amongst other measures, introduced the control of migration within the country, created one of the largest marine reserves in the world (c.130,000km²), prohibited industrial fishing and established institutions for participatory management of the Marine Reserve. The creation of the Galapagos Marine Reserve was the fruit of a local exhaustive participatory planning process, which took two years (74 meetings of a multi-stakeholder planning group called Grupo Núcleo, two fisheries summit meetings and three community workshops) and produced a consensus management plan. The implementation of this plan, through a legally based participatory management regime, has been in progress now for several years.

The Galapagos co-management institution essentially consists of a tri-polar arrangement (see figure 4.1) uniting a local Participatory Management Board (PMB), an Inter-institutional Management Authority (IMA) and the Galapagos National Park (GNP). The Participatory Management Board (PMB) is made up of the primary local stakeholders whilst the IMA comprises representatives of Ministers and local stakeholders. In the PMB, the members present specific management proposals (e.g. concerning regulations of fisheries and tourism), which are analysed, negotiated and eventually agreed upon by consensus. The consensus-based proposals are channelled for approval to the IMA and then to the GNP, for implementation and control. Proposals that have reached a consensus in the PMB carry an important weight at the IMA level. However, if no consensus is reached in the PMB, the different stakeholder positions are submitted to the IMA, where the decision is left in the hands of a majority of mainland ministerial officials. Statistics are compelling. Nearly 100% of consensus-based PMB proposals (which, incidentally, managed to secure excellent conservation results) are approved without modification in the IMA. Obviously, the consensus-based co-management setting creates a strong incentive for local stakeholders to develop and agree on viable proposals in the PMB.

Figure 4.1   Co-management structure for the Galapagos Marine Reserve
(for explanation of abbreviations, see Box 4.2)

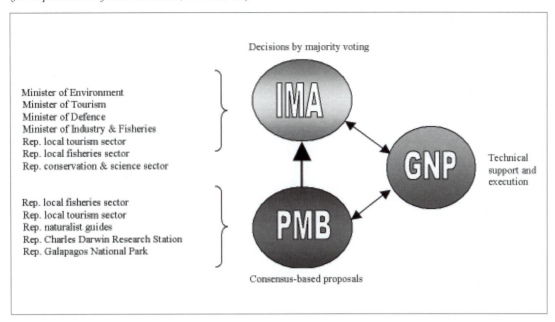

Among the most interesting co-management models are those that strongly combine local/traditional and western/"modern" policies and practices. Such cases include:

- Lands and resources traditionally belonging to indigenous or local communities that were incorporated within government-designated protected areas without the agreement of the concerned communities, though they later regained some form of community entitlement or jurisdiction (e.g. through court judgements). The communities and the government jointly set up co-management boards and develop regulations corresponding partially or totally to the government-designated protected area (see an example in Box 6.3).

- Lands and resources customarily set aside by indigenous and local communities under special management regulations and practices that were incorporated into government-designated protected areas with some form of recognition and maintenance of prior customary management. The communities and the government agreed on sharing management authority and responsibility through specific agreements, regulations and co-management boards corresponding partially or totally to the government-designated protected area (see an example in Box 4.3).

Characteristics of Government-managed and Co-managed Protected Areas

Co-managed Protected Areas can be analysed in various ways. Apart from the objectives of management (reflected in the IUCN management category) and governance arrangements (see Chapter 2), key distinguishing features are:

- Historical origin of the protected area (was the protected area imposed over the will of indigenous and local communities or were the communities in agreement with the establishment of the protected area and its key management objectives?

Box 4.3   Demanding co-management – the Kaa-ya Iya del Gran Chaco National Park (Bolivia)
(adapted from Beltrán, 2000;Winer, 2001; Winer, 2003)

The Kaa-ya Iya National Park (83.4 million hectares) is the largest in Bolivia and contains the world's largest area of dry tropical forest under legal protection. Another unique characteristic of this park is that it was created in response to demands for territorial recognition by the Guaraní Izoceño people. This is the first protected area in the Americas to be declared at the behest of the indigenous people, and it is the only park in the Americas where an indigenous peoples' organization (CABI – Capitanía del Alto y Bajo Izozog) has primary administrative responsibility. The Park's Management Committee comprises staff of the Ministry of Sustainable Development and Planning and representatives of CABI, WCS (a foreign environmental NGO), local municipalities, a community group of Chiquitanos, the Ayoreo Community of Santa Teresita and the group of women of the Izozog indigenous communities. The indigenous representatives are the majority in the Committee, which is in charge of several management policies and decisions.

In 1993, the new Agrarian Reform Law recognised Bolivia as a multi-ethnic and multi-cultural country, allowing for community land ownership and legalising the creation of indigenous territories (Territorio Comunitario de Origen – TCO). With the passing of this law, CABI and the indigenous communities could become fully involved in management of the park and address a number of conservation problems. In addition, CABI had been able to secure significant compensatory payments ($3.7 million) from industry for the impact of a gas pipeline that runs through their indigenous territory and the park. This and other income were invested by CABI in the running of the park, greatly strengthening their standing as co-management partners. The compensation funds have also supported the indigenous organizations themselves, promoted rural development and accelerated the titling of indigenous lands. The park's creation helped to halt the rapid expanse of the agro-industrial sector and ensured that vast expanses of traditional lands were not clear-cut for farming.

Were communities involved in asking for the protected area? Was any resettlement involved? Was there a negotiated compensation for any communities leaving their territories?).

- Length of time the governance model has been in place (has the Co-Managed Protected Area been in place for more or less than a decade? Has it been able to "adjust" its governance structure and procedures to the context?).

- Permission accorded or not accorded for people to inhabit the protected area or a designated buffer zone around it, and/or permission accorded or not accorded for people to carry out activities within the protected area or buffer zone.

- Extent of community interest in and engagement with the protected area (are community members aware of the existence of the protected area)? Is the protected area valued as a component of community identity, culture and livelihoods? Has the community demonstrated the will to participate in its management?

- Extent of government interest in and engagement with the protected area (is the area considered a major element in the national protected area system – a "jewel in the crown"? Is it endowed with sufficient human and financial resources?).

- Flexibility of the system (is the institutional setting prescribed by legislation, for instance regarding who should be the members of the management board, or is there room for adjustment and experimentation, responding to the specific characteristics of the context? Is adaptive management the overall approach?).

▪ Ecological performance (is the protected area effective in protecting biodiversity and critical ecological services? According to what indicators and whose monitoring results?).

▪ Social, cultural, and economic performance (is the protected area meeting the needs of local communities?).

In the case of Co-managed Protected Areas additional important characteristics, which are often difficult to assess, include:

▪ Fairness of process (is protected area governance supported by independent bodies or experts, capable of promoting and "watching over" the fairness of negotiations? In particular, is such support available to facilitate the development of specific agreements, multi-stakeholder management bodies, and/or good relationships between government agencies and communities? Are there specific forms of support to facilitate participation of under-privileged sectors of the community?).

▪ Adequacy of capacities and means (are the co-management structure and processes legally recognised and "secured" from the perspective of all its parties? Are the human and financial resources adequate to sustain the governance option, especially in its transaction-intensive initial phases? Is the income stream sufficient to sustain recurrent costs of social communication, negotiated decision-making, collective operations and monitoring?).

▪ Extent of power sharing and effective collaboration among the involved parties (e.g. governmental agencies, indigenous and local communities and other stakeholders).

The above list of characteristics does not describe all features of a protected area, or even of its relationship with local people. But it can be used to distinguish between "strong" and "weak" co-management models. For instance, a regional review in South-East Asia[90] identified some very weak and some less weak models. In Malaysia, Vietnam, Laos and Cambodia, protected area agencies have recently begun to involve concerned communities in the management of protected areas, but only for protected area buffer zones and surroundings. Similar developments are underway in West Africa, for example in Burkina Faso, Niger and Bénin. Such management participation is not codified in law and is left to the discretion of individual managers. Examples of a rather stronger co-management models are found in the Philippines, where each protected area is required by law to be run by a Management Board composed of government officers, NGOs and community representatives – though this has been hampered by a lack of documents in local languages, limited resources for meetings and workshops, and the common unwillingness of local people to voice their concerns in the presence of the chairperson of that board, who is appointed by the government.[91]

---

[90]   Ferrari, 2002.

[91]   Ferrari and De Vera, 2003.

In Australia, strong co-management arrangements for protected areas have been developed over the last twenty years, following legislation that recognised Aboriginal rights to land and natural resources. In 1981, Gurig National Park became the first jointly managed National Park in Australia; since then, further co-management arrangements have been developed for other parks in various states and territories, according to several models (see Table 4.1). Co-management represents a trade-off between the rights and interests of traditional owners and the rights and interests of government conservation agencies and the wider Australian community. In the most sophisticated arrangements, land ownership is transferred to Aboriginal people in exchange for the peoples' agreement that the area will remain under protected status as a national park for the foreseeable future and that responsibility for park management will be shared. Often, a key element in these arrangements is the use of leases or other legal mechanisms, under which the land for protection is simultaneously returned to Aboriginal ownership and leased back to a government conservation agency under a co-management board, with all parties committing to arbitration in case of disputes. The most recent form of protected area established voluntarily on existing Aboriginal-owned land – the Indigenous Protected Area described in Chapter 5 – is even more advanced in terms of self-determination and self-management by the Aboriginal owners.[92]

In Latin America, there has been a recent growth in experimentation with models where civil society and state share responsibility for protected area management, with numerous inspiring examples,[93] in particular in the Andean region. In Central America, 79 cases have been analysed,[94] revealing a variety of management types that take advantage of the relatively dynamic and open state of legislation and policies in the region.

Elsewhere, some states have legislation that works against co-management. For instance, Swedish legislation requires the state to buy the land from the legal owners before a national park can be declared; yet the relationship with neighbouring communities remains important and protected area staff are requested to take it carefully into account in their work.[95] Several countries, such as Argentina, the Democratic Republic of Congo, Germany, India, Iran and Romania are in an "experimental" stage of co-management. Others, such as Australia, Bolivia, Canada, France, Italy, the Philippines and the UK, have already accepted and recognised co-management as a valuable and effective model.

Some common features of Co-managed Protected Areas

Before turning to the options for co-management, it is useful to reflect on the key features that are common to all co-management arrangements:

- Co-management is an arena of social engagement, encounter and experimentation. Many protected area co-management arrangements are relatively new, and

---

[92] So much so that it actually is a CCA rather than a Co-managed Protected Area.

[93] Oviedo, 2002.

[94] Solis Rivera *et al.*, 2003.

[95] Gunnar Zettersten, personal communication, 2002.

Table 4.1 Four management 'models' in Australia
(adapted from Smyth, 2001)

Gurig model	Uluru model	Queensland model	Witjira model
Aboriginal ownership	Aboriginal ownership	Aboriginal ownership	Ownership of land remains with the government
Equal representation of traditional owners and government representatives on board of management	Aboriginal majority on board of management	No guarantee of Aboriginal majority on board of management	Aboriginal majority on board of management
No lease-back to governmentAgency	Lease-back to government agency for long period	Lease-back to government agency in perpetuity	Lease of the national park to traditional owners
Annual fee to traditional owners	Annual fee to traditional owners, community council or board	No annual fee paid	
Example: Gurig National Park	Examples: Uluru-Kata Tjuta, Kakadu, Nitmiluk, Booderee and Mutawintji National Parks	Examples: none finalised	Example: Witjira National Park

even those that have had one or several decades of experimentation are still exploring structures and options. As such, they are interesting arenas for learning and change. It is often sensible to adopt a flexible and adaptive approach while the various players adjust themselves to the new arrangements.

■ Co-management capitalizes on multiplicity and diversity. Co-management is usually a multi-party but also a multi-level and multi-disciplinary endeavour. Different social actors possess different capacities and contribute different strengths to management. A partnership stresses and builds upon these complementary roles. Different social actors, however, may also possess contrasting interests and concerns. The challenge is to create a situation in which the pay-offs for everyone are greater when collaboration occurs rather than competition.

■ Co-management is based upon a negotiated, joint decision-making approach and some degree of power-sharing, sharing of responsibilities, and distribution of benefits among all institutional actors. While the type and extent of power-sharing and benefit distribution vary from situation to situation, all actors acquire *some* voice and receive *some* benefits from their involvement. This fact alone may help to empower the least powerful stakeholders, thus redressing societal imbalances and fostering social justice.

■ Co-management is more of a flexible process than a stable and definitive end point. It requires on-going review and improvement rather than the strict application of a set of rules. Its most important result is not a management plan but a management partnership, capable of responding to varying circumstances and needs. And co-management agreements and organizations have a healthy tendency to evolve. This allows them to strive towards ever more effective and equitable arrangements and to maintain the liveliness and flexibility to respond to change.

Options for action and advice

Agencies managing or co-managing protected areas have a number of options for action that they can take to enhance effectiveness and equity. Basic to all these options is the recognition that, where protected areas affect the livelihoods and interests of local communities, it is important to gain their support if protected areas are to achieve their conservation aims. Furthermore, it is increasingly recognised that it is unacceptable for protected areas to dis-empower or impoverish their resident communities. These points were emphasised at the 2003 World Parks Congress in Durban,[96] enshrined in its Recommendations and later re-affirmed by the 2004 CBD Programme of Work on Protected Areas.[97]

The process of engaging communities as management partners should ideally begin at the stage of planning and design, encourage the effective participation of all interested parties at every stage, and provide meaningful responses to their concerns. The key options for action for this (see below) can actually be seen as *steps* in this process, as one often depends on the fair accomplishment of the other. By adopting a positive approach to the involvement of local communities, a national protected area agency and/or a local protected area administration can "move along the continuum" of Figure 3.1 and develop stronger co-management models. Each model, however, should be tailored to the unique circumstances of the relevant country and communities.[98]

4.1 Share information, advice and conservation benefits with the concerned communities

The sharing of information, advice and benefits is the *first and essential step* to be taken in any management setting: it can be considered as the "foundation" for co-management.

4.1.1 Consult with relevant communities regarding the need for, objectives and management priorities of any new protected area

Too often, protected areas have been declared without consultation with communities who are traditionally associated with the area and its resources. This was almost invariably the case in the past and is still quite common. Yet, such consultations should take place well in advance of setting up any new protected area. The consultations should address the need for, objectives, management priorities, foreseen arrangements and any other important aspect of the proposed protected area. According to what is socially and culturally appro-priate, they may involve public hearings, focus group meetings with specific sectors of the communities, mail and phone-based questionnaires, open debates in the local press, and the like. The necessary documents for meaningful consultation need to be provided to the communities in advance and in local languages. Oral means of information need to be stressed wherever formal literacy is low. Eventually, a consultation process should produce a broad social consensus on whether or not to establish the protected area, and – if so – what should be its main objectives, its management priorities, etc.

---

[96] Cernea and Schmidt-Soltau, 2003; Brockington, 2003.

[97] For instance in Activity 2.1.1 of goal 2.1 and activity 2.2.5 of goal 2.2.

[98] Some Community Conserved Areas are also moving along the continuum of Figure 3.1, but in the opposite direction (from right to left)! In this case, the relevant communities engage state agencies and other parties to contribute to the management of the areas and resources of concern to them, e.g. through novel contractual agreements and/or the inscription of customary rights in national legislation.

4.1.2 Consult with relevant communities on the technical decisions about protected areas

Protected area agencies often assign to professional staff and experts the task of developing technical documents, such as management plans, zoning arrangements, specific regulations and prohibitions, the range of permitted activities in the protected area, etc. While such decisions are under consideration – and also after they are taken – staff may wish to hear the views of the relevant stakeholders. It is therefore necessary to disseminate relevant information and set a period of time for comments and suggested changes. In this option, the agency takes this feedback into account while maintaining full authority for final decisions, which is often considered convenient by several parties. The management agency has only the burden of disseminating information fairly, while other actors can make their view known with the minimum investment of time. Problems with the option concern the lack of effective power sharing and the lack of a "space" where different actors can speak with one another and develop new ideas in an articulated, negotiated mode. In other words, this option may "defuse" conflicts but has little chance of tackling them in substantial and durable ways.[99]

4.1.3 Share protected area information promptly and fully though social communication events that allow open discussion and mutual learning

Even the most basic type of involvement depends on information. Logically, then, if indigenous and local communities are to be positively engaged, they must be well-informed about the protected areas of concern to them. Protected area policy makers and staff should provide them with official and "scientific" information on the area's characteristics and values, the factors affecting these, current management objectives and governance regimes, relevant legislation, policies and by-laws, the rights and responsibilities conferred on different parties, and how affected parties can express their interests, concerns and grievances, as well as how they may themselves make proposals.

But information should not flow in one direction only. Managing agencies should not assume that they hold all the facts about the protected area, but rather use social communication methodologies and information sharing as opportunities for mutual learning. Indigenous communities, for example, may know more than formal biologists about the socio-economic situation in an area, may have a wealth of observational data, and may make significant contributions to biological monitoring and surveillance that can assist protected area staff. A positive attitude and versatility in any local languages on the part of protected area staff are also important. What are needed are opportunities for staff and local people to listen to one another, even across knowledge systems and ways of communicating. Social communication events and venues provide occasions for people not only to receive information but also to share it, discuss it and make sense of it in a collective way.

---

[99] A fuller account of this "consultation option" in connection with management planning is set out in Chapter 5 of *Guidelines for Management Planning of Protected Areas* (Thomas and Middleton, 2003).

> **Box 4.4   First steps towards collaborative management of Retezat National Park (Romania)**
> (adapted from Stanciu, 2001)
>
> A small area of outstanding beauty and biodiversity – 100km² of untouched forest and alpine areas within the Retezat Massif – was declared a National Park in 1935. The area around the park is rich in natural and cultural resources and the local people are largely engaged in traditional agriculture. Romanian and foreign visitors travel to this remote area mostly in the summer. The Retezat National Park Management Authority (PMA) was established in November 1999 with the help of a GEF-supported biodiversity conservation project. Early in 2000, the park area was enlarged and a stakeholder analysis was undertaken. In 2001, a Consultative Council was established, with 25 representatives from the main interests concerned: local communities, forest districts, NGOs, mountain rescue teams, school inspectorates, local scientific bodies and county level institutes. All important management decisions are supposed to be made only after consulting the Council and, if necessary, the public at large.
>
> During the first meetings of the Council, short training sessions were held on participatory approaches and "how to work together". The local people are the bearers of the cultural and traditional values of the area, which contribute much to the landscape and biodiversity of the national park, so their understanding and collaboration are essential. But the participatory approach is new to them, and quite different from that adopted under the former communist administration. To develop local peoples' confidence in a more participatory role, a "learning by doing" route has been taken by the PMA.

4.1.4   Share protected area benefits with relevant communities through ways and means proposed by protected area agencies

Protected areas generate both costs and benefits, which should be, in a general sense, equitably distributed. One limited but still powerful way of engaging communities in conservation is the distribution of benefits to them, including economic benefits from gate fees, other tourism-related revenues, jobs for local people and access to natural resources on a preferential basis. As important to local stakeholders as these economic benefits are, local people often attach more importance to the spiritual and cultural values associated with a protected area's land and resources, the social and/or legal recognition of their rights, the opportunity to participate in decision-making, and considerations of livelihood security.[100]

The type and extent of benefit sharing can be proposed, decided upon and controlled by protected area authorities and administered primarily as a form of "compensation" for costs incurred and impacts felt by certain stakeholders.[101] When undertaken in this manner, benefit sharing may be effective but rather paternalistic, engaging communities as "beneficiaries" rather than partners, and its sustainability in the long term and under changing conditions is questionable. In more participatory models, the sharing of costs and benefits arising from protected areas is established through a negotiated agreement among stakeholders and protected area authorities (see options under 4.3 below).

---

[100]   Harmon, 2003.

[101]   See, for instance, Okello *et al.*, 2003 and Baldus *et al.*, 2003.

4.2 Empower indigenous peoples and local and mobile communities to participate in protected area management

A *second step* towards co-management is the strengthening of communities through a process of analysing the relevant issues, leading to self-organising and capacity building according to their needs.[102] Indigenous and local communities and their organizations may require new capacities and resources to be able to relate effectively to government agencies and conservation NGOs in formal settings, and to assume new roles and responsibilities. Similarly policy makers and on-the-ground staff of conservation agencies may also benefit from training and support in working with indigenous and local communities (see sections 4.4.1 and 6.4).

4.2.1 Engage communities in assessing the biological and social situation of the protected area at stake and developing a joint vision of its desired future

Provision of information through written materials, briefings or even discussion sessions may not be sufficient to arouse the interest of communities and their willingness to adopt conservation action. A more empowering way to engage communities is through participatory assessment and visioning exercises, examples of which have been used with success in many countries and communities.[103] The methods generally encourage a process by which local communities analyse the conditions, problems and opportunities they face, sketch the future they desire for themselves and subsequent generations, explore strategies to reach that future and address options and threats along the way. In this process, external experts with information on possible threats to the local natural resource base, and to other biological and ecological trends, can be seen as allies, and not as outsiders attempting to use environmental scare tactics on local stakeholders. These exercises can be initiated regardless of the legal and policy situation, but their effectiveness is stronger if people feel confident that the results of their community assessments and visioning exercises will be seriously considered and respected. Participatory processes such as these can become the foundation of long-term alliances for sound natural resource management.[104] They should not, however, be taken lightly. Engaging a community in a difficult and engrossing process and then ignoring the results of consultation can be a recipe for later conflict.

4.2.2 Support communities to organize and build their capacities, as they see fit

Communities and other non-institutionalized actors may need support to organize themselves effectively and engage with others in decisions and action. It is not always

---

[102] The process of strengthening communities for an effective role in negotiation and some lessons learned thereby has been recently summarised by Borrini-Feyerabend *et al.*, 2004 (in press).

[103] For instance, the tribes of Matavén in the Orinoco region of Colombia have had a chance to go though some facilitated internal participatory processes and develop their "life plans". This has been an empowering experience for them, which they have used to guide any subsequent interaction with local, regional and national governments. The "life plans" are based on the history of the indigenous group and on traditional, elders' knowledge. On those bases, the communities develop a vision of their desired future and identify a path towards achieving it – their "life plan", which is a local agenda, dealing with health, education, identity preservation and sound environmental management. For the Matavén people, the agenda explicitly includes a combination of sustainable use and preservation of territories and resources (Luque, 2003).

[104] For an extensive library and links on participatory rural appraisal methods, see www.eldis.org/participation and http://nrm.massey.ac.nz/changelinks   For information on community mapping methods, see Poole, 1995; Momberg *et al.* 1996; Barton *et al.*, 1997.

the case that a community is clear about all of its interests and concerns regarding the establishment or management of a protected area and/or its relation to it. This may be due to a lack of information or even lack of time or opportunity to discuss the issues and agree on how to get themselves "represented" in discussions with others. NGOs may claim to speak for local communities, self-appointed leaders may claim to speak for their peoples, or an industry owner may claim to speak on behalf of a whole economic sector, but such "representation" should always be independently verified. Even when protected areas' authorities have "consulted" with a local or indigenous community, they may have used a route that the community does not recognise – a fact that can easily give rise to problems.

It would therefore be better if independent bodies, such as an NGO or, exceptionally, the protected area agency itself, provided encouragement, facilitation, technical advice and financial support to help the communities to organize themselves and avoid speaking on their behalf to the maximum extent. In this, they can help by assisting communities to meet, discuss issues, decide on priorities and a strategy to follow, identify their representatives, facilitate input from *all* community members, perhaps acquire a legal status as a local association, and establish records, lines of communication, a regular meeting place and so forth. An example of community-representative association that effectively negotiated a co-management plan is provided in Box 4.5. As part of the organising process, it is likely that the communities also identify what new capacities they need, ranging from literacy, numeracy and basic management skills to legal support to develop a recognised community association with the necessary powers.

Overcoming time and travel constraints is a mundane but important element of capacity building for many stakeholders. Participation can be expensive for local and indigenous communities (as it is for local officials of poorly funded protected area agencies and local government units!). Travel can be difficult, time-consuming and/or expensive, particularly in the remote rural regions. Taking time off from work to attend meetings is not an option for many rural people unless the process is designed with their particular needs in mind. So it is best to avoid scheduling meetings during harvest time, key fishing times or religious and cultural events. Another step may be to reimburse travel costs for all parties that cannot afford them on their own: for example, in the Inuvialut Final Agreement for Co-management of the Canadian Western Arctic, the costs of indigenous peoples' participation are covered for attending meetings.[105]

4.3 Engage the concerned communities in negotiation processes and management institutions

This *third step* signals a significant change: moving from a situation in which protected area agencies are "in charge", to one in which authority and responsibilities are effectively shared.

4.3.1 Integrate local/traditional and national/modern practices and knowledge

In areas with strong traditions of natural resource management by indigenous peoples and local and mobile communities, successful co-management models integrate local/

---

[105]   Larsen, 2000.

44

Box 4.5   The Dayak people co-manage the Kayan Mentarang National Park: a first in Indonesia!
(adapted from Ferrari, 2002; Eghenter and Labo, 2003)

The Kayan Mentarang National Park (KMNP) situated in the interior of East Kalimantan (Indonesian Borneo) lies at the border with Sarawak to the west and Sabah to the north. With 1.4 million ha, it is the largest protected area of rainforest in Borneo and one of the largest in Southeast Asia. The history of the landscape of the park is intertwined with that of its people. About 16,000 Dayak people live inside or near the park. These are still communities largely regulated by customary law, or *adat,* in the conduct of their daily affairs and the management of natural resources in their customary territory (*wilayah adat)*. The chief (*kepala adat*) and council (*lembaga adat*) administer the customary law. All elected officials at village level and prominent leaders of the community are members of the customary council, which declare traditional forest areas with protection status or strict management regime. These are referred to as *tana ulen,* i.e. land to which access is restricted. Such lands cover primary forest rich in natural resources, such as rattan (*Calamus* spp.), sang leaves (*Licuala* sp.), hardwood for construction (e.g., *Dipterocarpus* spp., *Shorea* spp., *Quercus* sp.), fish and game, all of which have high use value for the local community.

In 1980, the area was established as a Nature Reserve, under a strict protection status that allowed no human activity. Later on, a study that included community mapping exercises showed that the Dayak communities had rightful claims to the land and its resources. This study recommended a change of status from Nature Reserve to National Park, where traditional activities are allowed. A WWF project identified the lack of tenure security as a major concern: this had transformed the Dayak's forest into an "open access forest", where the state could decide to allocate exploitation rights or establish a conservation regime without their prior consent. Because of this, the Dayak communities had little power to defend the forest or secure their economic livelihoods against logging companies, mining exploration, or outside collectors of forest products. The project therefore decided to help the Dayak to obtain the recognition of *adat* claims and *adat* rights, so that indigenous communities could continue to use and manage forest resources in the protected area. From 1996 to 2000, the project helped them in a number of tasks, including biological and economic inventories, participatory planning workshops (to identify precisely the *tana ulen* forests, and include this knowledge in zoning recommendations), redrawing the boundaries of the park, compiling and recording their customary rules, strengthening their own organizations, etc.

The Alliance of the Indigenous People of Kayan Mentarang National Park (FoMMA) was formally established on October 2000 by the leaders of the ten customary lands of the park. This created a forum for indigenous communities to debate issues and convey their views on the management of natural resources in the customary lands of the KMNP. FoMMA is concerned with guaranteeing protection of the forest and the sustainable use of natural resources in the ten customary lands of the national park area, as well as with the protection of the rights of indigenous people and their economic prosperity in and around the park area. FoMMA now legally represents the concerned indigenous people in the Policy Board (Dewan Penentu Kebijakan), a new institution set up to preside over the park's management. The Policy Board includes representatives of the central government (the agency for Forest Protection and Nature Conservation), the provincial and district governments and FoMMA. The operating principles of the board emphasise coordination, competence, shared responsibilities, and equal partnership among all stakeholders. The board was formally established in April 2002 with a Decree of the Ministry of Forestry, which officially declared Kayan Mentarang National Park to be managed through this collaborative arrangement.

traditional and national/"modern" systems, policies and practices. The first step is for protected area agencies to study and document community conservation values, knowledge, skills, resources and institutions. Such studies should not be undertaken lightly or superficially, as local cultures are often sophisticated, complex and very different from each other in terms of values and belief systems. The results of the studies should be discussed among the concerned parties, beginning with the holders of traditional knowledge themselves. It is important to examine how the results of the studies can best be taken into account in planning and decision-making, for example whether and how the local traditional natural resource management systems can be adapted and/or merged with conventional "scientific" knowledge, resources and institutions to solve the concrete problems faced by each protected area. In this context, practical solutions speak more than many lofty declarations of intent.

4.3.2 Negotiate co-management plans and complementary agreements with communities and other parties

Communities can be involved in decision making in various ways, from being part of a technical body authorized to develop protected area plans, rules and regulations, to being members of the protected area management board in charge of deciding upon and implementing such rules. A multi-party forum is essential for communication, dialogue and consensual decisions. The persons or organizations convening and facilitating the negotiation process[106] must be skilled and perceived as fair. If the convener or facilitator is viewed as biased towards the interests of one of the parties, the process may lose credibility. The convener or facilitator should draw upon a variety of flexible mechanisms for negotiating agreement, such as detailed zoning for conservation and resource use, detailed conditions for allowed resource use, leases, compensation arrangements, complementary projects, financial incentives, etc. The ability to manage and resolve controversies through mediation and effective compromise is invaluable.

In some cases, the controversies that engulf protected area agencies and indigenous and local communities are so serious and longstanding that it may be better to engage in formal legal proceedings, or to take the case before a tribunal, a human rights body or a Truth and Reconciliation Commission. Such proceedings should not be feared but actually promoted by agency staff, since a festering conflict may be much more disruptive in the long run than a difficult but fair court judgement.

Negotiation of co-management plans and complementary accords is not limited to a one-time-only event, but should be seen an ongoing process in which protected area staff, communities and other legitimate stakeholders plan and implement activities together and learn by doing. As part of this, the costs and benefits of establishing and managing a protected area should be assessed. Then a fairer and more sustainable balance should be reflected in appropriate policies in subsequent co-management plans and complementary agreements.

---

[106] The process of negotiating co-management agreements for natural resources and the lessons learned thereby have been recently summarised in Part II of Borrini-Feyerabend *et al.*, 2004 (in press).

The Regole d'Ampezzo manage a Community Conserved Area with a recorded history of approximately 1,000 years. Today, they have been recognized as sole managers of the Regional Natural Park declared on their common lands, have been granted tax-free status from the Italian government, and have secured project funds and subsidies from the European Union and other public sources. See also Box 5.3. *(Courtesy Stefano Lorenzi and Regole d'Ampezzo)*

The Executive Director of TIDE – which manages a Community Conserved Area in Belize called Port Honduras Marine Reserve – proudly shows the excellent catches achieved with sustainable fishing rules. *(Courtesy TIDE)*

Children in the Kaa-Iya del Gran Chaco National Park. Kaa-Iya is the largest park in Bolivia, includes the largest area of dry tropical forest under full-protected area status anywhere in the world and owes its existence to an indigenous organisation's efforts to consolidate its territorial claims through the creation of a protected area. See also Box 4.3. *(Courtesy Hal Noss)*

The Capitanía de Alto y Bajo Izozog (CABI), representing some 9,500 Guaraní Izoceños living in 25 communities along the Parapetí river, now co-manages with the Bolivian government the 3.4 million hectare Kaa-Iya del Gran Chaco National Park, which guarantees the physical and cultural integrity of the Guaraní Izoceños' resource base. *(Courtesy Hal Noss)*

Leaders from various ethnic groups gathered in Yurayaco–Caquetá, Colombia. The Alto Fragua Indiwasi National Park was proposed by the Ingano peoples and is now managed according to their own shamanic rules. See also Box 5.2. *(Courtesy Asociación de Cabildos Tandachiridu Inganokuna – Jose Ignacio Giraldo)*

A panoramic view of the Alto Fragua Indiwasi National Park, Colombia. Biodiversity conservation depends on the engagement of the people living with the natural resources, whose cultural diversity, in turn, depends on access to those resources and the capacity to maintain their traditional livelihoods. *(Courtesy Asociación de Cabildos Tandachiridu Inganokuna – Jose Ignacio Giraldo)*

The Bijagos biosphere reserve (Guinea Bissau) includes numerous areas (e.g. entire islands) strictly protected according to local ancestral rules. On the basis of those rules the state subsequently declared official protected areas. In a number of cases, the communities are entirely in charge of their management plans and activities (see also the picture on the front cover). *(Courtesy Grazia Borrini-Feyerabend)*

Women returning home from the fields in Krayan Hulu, Kayan Mentarang National Park—the first national park to be granted official collaborative management status in Indonesia (April 2002). By carefully collecting edible plants from the forest, women contribute to community livelihood through sustainable use of wild plants. See also Box 4.5. (*Courtesy Cristina Eghenter*)

Most European protected areas were identified and declared based on cultural and spiritual attributes as well as ecological value. They are usually managed through complex collaborative agreements with landowners, communities and other concerned parties. See also Box 3.2. *(Courtesy Andy Wilson and North York Moors National Park Authority, UK)*.

The Chartang-Kushkizar wetland, extending some 9 km in length, has been since time immemorial conserved by two Qashqai sub-tribes of indigenous mobile pastoralists: the Kuhi and the Kolahli. The wetland is in the process of being officially recognized by the Iranian government as a Community Conserved Area. See also Box 5.5. *(Courtesy Ahmad Reza Siapoosh)*

Certain wildlife species are sacred to local people throughout West Africa. Crocodiles, for instance, are nearly invariably respected. Crocodile ponds can be found at times very close to villages, despite the risks they represent to people and, especially, small children. Here is an example from Mali, at the border with Burkina Faso. *(Courtesy Grazia Borrini-Feyerabend)*

The farmed countryside of the island of Minorca (Spain) is a mosaic of meadows rich in wild flowers, enlaced by stone walls and stone-edged waterways. Grazing creates the conditions for biodiversity to be maintained and the local breed of cows is part of the island's heritage. A satisfied cow owner has his farm well set inside the Albufera del Grau Nature Park, the core of the local biosphere reserve. *(Courtesy Grazia Borrini-Feyerabend)*

Coron Island, in the Philippines, is part of the ancestral domain of the Tagbanwa people, only recently legally recognized. The Tagbanwa strive to manage their natural resources in a sustainable way. Their forest products are used only for domestic needs, fishing is regulated, and all the freshwater lakes in the island but one are sacred and cannot be utilized for any reason, and especially not for tourism. *(Courtesy Maurizio Farhan Ferrari)*

Tagbanwa people with the three-dimensional map they created of their own island. The production of this map helped them to obtain an official Certificate of Ancestral Domain Claim. *(Courtesy Maurizio Farhan Ferrari)*

Community people help to build an elephant trench outside Kibale National Park, Uganda. The Park has entered into a number of formal agreements with surrounding communities, which allow people access to selected natural resources under certain conditions. In return, the communities monitor and protect those resources. *(Courtesy Purna Chhetri)*

Several villagers in Maharashtra (India) have initiated "study circles" (*abhyas gats*) on subjects such as forest-based rights or local biodiversity. In Mendha-Lekha this brought powerfully to light the long-term damages of commercial exploitation to the local forests and the need to conserve traditional seeds and agro-practices. *(Courtesy Ashish Kothari)*.

4.3.3 Develop and support a co-management institution capable of responding through time to the changing needs of a protected area and its relevant management partners

A protected area management institution is generally based on a set of rules (e.g. a management plan, including zoning and detailed conditions of resource use) and one or more organizations in charge of developing, interpreting and implementing such rules on an on-going basis, responding to varying circumstances and needs. In a co-management setting, such bodies comprise, in a more or less formal way, representatives of the government staff, the indigenous and local communities and all other relevant stakeholders.[107] In identifying the composition of these bodies, it is important that a fair distinction is made between stakeholders and rights-holders. For instance, indigenous peoples and the local and mobile communities who traditionally owned, occupied or used lands and resources within a protected area may claim customary and/or legal rights to such lands and resources based on ancient possession, continuity of relationship, historical ties, cultural ties and direct dependency on the resources. It would not be right to assign to them and to other interested groups (e.g. newcomers and opportunistic resource users) "equal weight" in decision-making institutions or for the purpose of benefit sharing. Criteria, such as those listed in Box 4.1, help to distinguish between primary and other stakeholders and rights-holders. A successful example of giving priority in the management to those with long standing rights is given in Box 4.5.

Co-management organizations come in all shapes and sizes, with different mandates, regulations and characteristics. Many lessons about their effectiveness and sustainability have been derived from accumulated experience.[108] For example, the form of such bodies should be developed through a negotiation process rather than prescribed in a top-down fashion or according to a pre-determined format. It is also known that they work best when they are rather small, internally diverse, and fully accountable; that they require time to develop an effective internal dialogue; and that a wise balance is needed between flexibility and "social experimentation" on the one hand, and having rules that are respected and enforced on the other. Overall, the most important characteristic of co-management institutions seems to be their own orientation to learning and capacity to learn. All of the above can be sought after and nurtured by the agencies in charge.

4.3.4 As appropriate, negotiate the restitution of land and resources to the rightful indigenous peoples and local and mobile communities or devolve management authority and responsibility to them

In a number of countries it has been possible in the past to impose protected areas status on territories inhabited by indigenous and local communities without any form of consultation, agreement or compensation. Today, some such countries are engaged in processes of land restitution to the relevant communities, the result of governmental changes, as in South Africa, or court decisions that made it illegal to remain in the *status quo*, as in Australia. Political or financial decentralization and devolution

---

[107] Note that this may not be relevant where multiple stakeholders or rightsholders do not exist, e.g. in a remote uninhabited island managed only by government agencies, or a completely community-owned and managed area.

[108] See Part III of Borrini-Feyerabend *et al.*, [in press].

Box 4.6   Gwaii Haanas: a successful example of co-management from Canada
(adapted from Gladu *et al.*, 2003)

In the Haida language, *gwaii haanas* means "islands of wonder and beauty". The Gwaii Haanas National Park Reserve, located within the Queen Charlotte Islands off the coast of British Columbia, was established in 1986 under an agreement between Parks Canada and the Council of the Haida Nation. The Haida themselves initiated the process, after their land and culture started to disappear due to heavy logging in their traditional territories. Through alliances with conservation organizations, the Haida people drew international attention to the spectacular beauty and diversity of their homeland and the need to protect it. The dual Park-Reserve status stems from the land ownership dispute. Both the government of Canada and the Haida claim ownership of the land. Fortunately, both sides have been able to put aside their differences regarding ownership and promote instead their common interests and goals. The Haida intent is to protect the area from environmental harm and degradation and continue traditional resource uses. The federal government's intent is to protect the area as a natural cultural environment as part of the national protected area system. Such objectives are perfectly compatible, leading to a relationship based on respect, reciprocity, empowerment and effective cooperation. In fact, Gwaii Haanas is now governed by a joint Management Board, made up of two Haida representatives and two Parks Canada representatives, working by consensus. This may slow down some decisions but assures that they are all well thought out and widely accepted.

The connection between land and culture is vital for the Haida, who are dependent on the natural resources for livelihood (through fishing, hunting and trapping) but also for medicines and the expression of their cultural identity through art. Five heritage sites within the borders of Gwaii Haanas are of particular high value to the Haida and are carefully protected. All this has been recognised and supported by Parks Canada. Consultation during the establishment and management of the protected area was adequate, and the process was not rushed (it took five years to come to an agreement). The establishment of the Park has promoted a shift in the local economy from logging to tourism. Employment opportunities have also been created by the park (more than 50% of park staff is Haida people). The only remaining challenge is to acknowledge the Haida presence, rights and participation in the management of the boundary waters of Gwaii Haanas. To the Haida, there is no separation of land and sea. Parks Canada, on the other hand, is promoting new federal legislation that could disrupt the Haida Nation's ability to move freely between the land and the sea by introducing different levels of protection for various areas and restricting the fishing rights in some of those areas.

processes are also underway in many countries, and these offer opportunities for governmental agencies and communities to work together in new and effective ways. Provided that respect, communication and some viable economic options exist, restitution, recognition and devolution of community rights may signal positive rather than negative conservation outcomes (see Box 6.3). Such outcomes, however, do not arise overnight, but occur only when the transfer of rights has been appropriately prepared, promoted, negotiated and supported by the agencies relinquishing control over land and resources.

In some cases, land and resource restitution may be accompanied by support to communities so that they can set up their own forms of conservation. This is the most advanced form of involving communities in conservation – empowering them to decide and act independently. Indigenous and local communities are then no longer mere participants in initiatives initiated and controlled by protected area staff or other stakeholders, but autonomous and responsible actors, who utilise a variety of means to initiate, develop and run their own conservation initiatives and decide themselves whether or not to take advantage of the incentives and forms of support the government may provide. Such independent initiatives, now known as "Community Conserved Areas", are the subject of Chapter 5 in these Guidelines.

4.4 Promote learning at various levels

On-going learning is the necessary *fourth step* and a crucial component of adaptive management, vital in protected areas which include some of the most precious and valuable environments and resources.

4.4.1 Enhance awareness and relevant technical capacities of protected area staff

Some agency staff appreciate the benefits that collaborative relationships with indigenous peoples and local and mobile communities could *eventually* bring about, but may be overwhelmed by what they perceive as the complexities, the challenging demands and long-term nature of the related efforts. If a protected area has existed for some time, it is likely to be set on well-established practices and may be resistant to new ideas, in particular regarding power sharing. If a protected area has yet to be established, the most pressing need of politicians may be to expedite decisions, for instance to sign an agreement with international donors, and not to set aside the time and resources for social communication, negotiation meetings and reaching a consensus with the local affected parties. When this happens, indigenous and local communities may be thought of as an obstacle or threat to conservation rather than as entitled actors with their own capacities, priorities and values.

Even when professionals are sincerely interested and concerned, scarce technical and human capacities may still block effective collaboration. In particular, too few protected area staff are properly trained to relate to people rather than to ecosystems, wildlife and infrastructures. Addressing this will call for capacity building initiatives, including training, over the long term. These need to begin from revised basic curricula for natural resource managers (see option 6.4.1). In continuing education initiatives, this could include conventional training sessions, in particular to raise awareness of community conservation values, knowledge, skills, resources and institutions (see also option 4.3.1). In general, however, field-based learning, exchanges among professionals engaged in similar processes, and "learning by doing" on the job (see option 4.4.2) are the most effective. Manuals and guidelines at the disposal of protected area staff should also specifically refer to the rational and appropriate methods of engaging various stakeholders in conservation.[109]

4.4.2 Promote "learning by doing" by all stakeholders in each protected area and mutual learning and sharing of experiences among protected areas in similar circumstances

Adaptive management emphasises on-going learning through iterative processes and fitting solutions to specific contexts. It is based on systematic experimentation and

---

[109] An example is Borrini-Feyerabend *et al.*, 2004 (in press).

careful analysis of feedback to management interventions and policies. A co-management regime ought to follow its tenets: the more the co-management actors invest in joint learning processes, the more their collaboration becomes relevant and effective. Institutional learning benefits from relationships based on mutual respect, a non-threatening environment, sound experimentation, critical thinking skills, and skills in recording, applying and disseminating lessons. All of these can be fostered at an individual protected area level through participatory monitoring and evaluation exercises; and it can be encouraged through a management attitude of openness to learning.

Shared learning among sites with similar circumstances, needs and opportunities is particularly effective and beneficial. Networking, exchange visits, and opportunities to share experiences and advice are a great element of support for both conservation agency staff and their partners, most of all the representatives of communities engaged in Co-managed Protected Areas. Learning networks, in particular, can be promoted at a landscape level among the managers of protected areas and Community Conserved Areas that benefit both from biological connectivity and from developing new lines of social and technical support. Such networks can be promoted at the national level, regionally and internationally, for instance to address bio-geographical concerns (e.g. the network of marine protected areas in West Africa or the network of Co-managed Protected Areas in the Congo Basin), to foster methodological exchanges (e.g. the network of professionals included in the IUCN/CEESP Co-management Working Group),[110] or to support exchange programmes that link protected areas in different regions.[111]

4.4.3   Facilitate participatory evaluation processes and protected area certification by international bodies

Involving protected area staff, communities and other relevant stakeholders in a review of protected area accomplishments and problems can help to clarify issues and identify opportunities for joint action. Most such reviews have dealt with environmental results, but they can also include governance practices and approaches (e.g. through the application of "good governance" criteria[112]). An interesting option, recently coming to the fore, regards regional or international review of the governance practices adopted in protected areas.[113] Such reviews would be oriented "positively" towards providing a label of quality to the best governed protected areas rather than singling out the ones that performed poorly. They represent a powerful avenue through which management effectiveness and good governance may become more widely understood and promoted for the benefit of all protected area parties.

---

[110]   See: www.iucn.org/themes/ceesp/Wkg_grp/CMWG/CMWG.htm Policies in support of national and international networking are discussed also in Chapter 6.

[111]   For a fuller account of the potential of protected area exchange programmes, see Hayes and Shultis, 2001.

[112]   See Chapter 2 and Graham *et al.*, 2003.

[113]   Abrams *et al.*, 2003.

5. Guidelines for Community Conserved Areas

In the early 2000s, the experience and concerns for conservation and equity that prompted the development of TILCEPA generated intense debates and exchanges, leading to the emergence of new conservation concepts. Among the most significant is that of the Community Conserved Area, which introduces nothing new but recognises and seeks the legitimization of some of the oldest conservation experiences and practices in the world.[115] Community Conserved Areas have been defined as:

> "*natural and modified ecosystems, including significant biodiversity, ecological services and cultural values, voluntarily conserved by indigenous peoples and local and mobile communities through customary laws or other effective means*".

Community Conserved Areas have three essential characteristics:

- Some indigenous peoples and local and mobile communities are "concerned" about the relevant ecosystems – usually being related to them culturally and/or because of livelihoods.

- Such indigenous and local communities are the major players (and hold power) in decision making and implementation of decisions on the management of the ecosystems at stake, implying that some form of community authority exists and is capable of enforcing regulations.

- The voluntary management decisions and efforts of such communities lead towards the conservation of habitats, species, ecological services and associated cultural values, although the protection status may have been set up to meet a variety of objectives, not necessarily related to the conservation of biodiversity.

Although not all Community Conserved Areas may be classified as protected areas, all of them make an important contribution to conservation, and as such they require recognition and support from national governments and the conservation community, especially in cases where they face threats from different forces and when communities are in a situation of vulnerability.

Many Community Conserved Areas are based entirely on customary rules and agreements, with no intervention by government agencies, no relation to official policies and no incorporation in formal legislation. Indeed in some cases the community maintains a degree of confidentiality over the exact location, boundaries and resources; very often, Community Conserved Areas are informal arrangements and officially un-recognised. Their contribution to a country's conservation system therefore goes un-noticed and

---

[115] The definition below was crafted out of the TILCEPA-sponsored regional reviews commissioned in preparation of the 5th World Parks Congress, in 2003. The early documents discussing it are collected in www.iucn.org/themes/ceesp/Wkg_grp/TILCEPA/community.html.

unsupported. Official protected areas may have been established, knowingly or unknowingly, on top of pre-existing Community Conserved Areas, putting traditional practices and management systems at risk, without substituting effective new rules. This can have serious negative results for both the conservation status of the resources and the livelihoods of people.[116]

When existing Community Conserved Areas *are* officially recognised by the state, there are several possible consequences:

- recognition does not substantially reduce the autonomy and decision-making power of the local communities. The area's conservation status is strengthened and the community benefits from some legal authority to enforce its decisions (for instance, an ordinance for the control of fishing could be issued for an area that a local community has declared as its own marine sanctuary);

- recognition implies a significant degree of sharing of authority and responsibility with governmental agencies; this alters the governance situation and transforms the Community Conserved Area into a Co-managed Protected Area (see Chapter 4); or

- the situation is in flux, with the power relationship between the state and the indigenous peoples or local communities being negotiated on an *ad-hoc* basis.

Significant examples of state recognition of Community Conserved Areas include the Indigenous Protected Areas of Australia (IPAs – see Box 5.1) and the Alto Fragua-Indiwasi

---

Box 5.1   Indigenous Protected Areas – a new model for Australia
(adapted from Smyth, 2001)

A strong, officially-recognised Community Conserved Area model exists in Australia: 'Indigenous Protected Area' (IPA) – see www.ea.gov.au/indigenous/ipa/index.html

The first IPA was formally proclaimed in August 1998, over an Aboriginal-owned property called Nantawarrina in the northern Flinders Ranges of South Australia. Several more IPAs have been proclaimed since.

IPAs recognise that some Aboriginal landholders are prepared to "protect" their land, and part of the Australia National Reserve System, in return for government support. They can establish formal conservation agreements under state or territory legislation, or under Indigenous Law. Aboriginal landowners can use various legal mechanisms to control activities on their land, including local by-laws and privacy laws. The declaration of IPAs marked the first occasion when Aboriginal landowners voluntarily accepted protected area status over their land. Because the process is voluntary, Aboriginal people can choose the level of government involvement, the level of visitor access (if any) and the extent of development to meet their needs. In return for government assistance, Aboriginal owners of IPAs are required to develop a management plan and to make a commitment to manage their land (and/or waters and resources) with the goal of conserving its biodiversity values. IPAs are attractive to some Aboriginal land owners because they bring management resources without a loss of autonomy, provide public recognition of the natural and cultural values of Aboriginal land, and recognise the capacity of Indigenous Peoples to protect and nurture those values. IPAs are attractive to government conservation agencies because they effectively add to the nation's conservation estate without the need to acquire the land, and incur the cost of the infrastructure, staffing, housing, etc., required of a national park.

---

[116]   An example is given in Box 1.1.

Box 5.2   Alto Fragua-Indiwasi – the government of Colombia recognises a Community Conserved Area as National Park
(adapted from Oviedo, 2002; Zuluaga *et al.*, 2003)

The Alto Fragua-Indiwasi National Park was created in February 2002, after negotiations involving the Colombian government, the Association of Indigenous Ingano Councils and the Amazon Conservation Team, an environmental NGO focusing on projects to assist the Ingano Indians and other indigenous groups in the Amazon basin. The park is located on the piedmont of the Colombian Amazon on the headwaters of the Fragua River. Inventories conducted by Colombia's von Humboldt Institute showed that Indiwasi National Park – formally known in Spanish as Parque Natural Nacional Alto Fragua-Indiwasi – is part of a region that has the highest biodiversity in the country and is one of the top hotspots of the world. The site will protect various ecosystems of the tropical Andes, including highly endangered humid sub-Andean forests, endemic species such as the spectacled bear (*Tremarctos ornatus*), and sacred sites of unique cultural value.

Under the terms of the decree that created the park, the Ingano are the principal actors in its design and management. The area, whose name means "House of the Sun" in the Ingano language, is a sacred place for the indigenous communities. This is one of the reasons why traditional authorities have insisted that the area's management should be entrusted to them. Although several protected areas of Colombia share management responsibilities with indigenous and local communities, this is the first one where the indigenous people are fully in charge. The creation of Indiwasi National Park has been a long-time dream of the Ingano communities of the Amazon Piedmont, for whom it makes a natural part of their Life Plan (*Plan de Vida*), that is, a broader, long-term vision for the entirety of their territory and the region. In addition, the creation of the Park represents an historic precedent for the indigenous people of Colombia, as for the first time an indigenous community is fully recognised by the state as the principal actor in the design and management of an official protected area. It is all the more remarkable that this community-promoted refuge has been developed in a context of armed violence, drug trafficking, and many other social problems that affect surrounding areas.

National Park in Colombia (see Box 5.2) These are now fully integrated into the respective national protected area systems, and have similar characteristics to other official protected areas in terms of size, ecological condition, and management objectives, although they are managed primarily by the relevant communities. The protected area system of most other countries, on the other hand, does not yet appear to "include" or take full advantage of the community protected ecosystems for conservation aims (see Box 5.3).

Some Community Conserved Areas involve lands traditionally belonging to indigenous or rural communities that in the past were incorporated into government property and now, through a variety of processes, are being "restituted".[117] These processes may give way to various forms of co-management agreements and institutions (see Chapter 4 and also Box 6.3). In other cases, the relevant communities strive for full state recognition of their own Community Conserved Area regime, which would allow them more autonomous decision-making power (see Box 5.4).

National governments generally establish and manage protected areas with conservation objectives in mind. On the other hand, many indigenous and local communities tend to establish their own conserved areas (or enter into a partnership to manage protected

---

[117]   MacKay (2002) reports instances of land restitutions in Australia, New Zealand, South Africa and the USA.

53

Box 5.3   Italian traditional institutions support healthy landscapes and wealthy communities
(adapted from Merlo *et al.*, 1989; Jeanrenaud, 2001;www.magnificacomunitafiemme.it; Stefano Lorenzi, personal communication, 2004; www.regole.it)

Long-established traditions of community forestry and pasture management in the north of Italy date from the Middle Ages and some can be traced to well before the Roman conquest. In some places, such as the Fiemme Valley, the community control over forests was maintained thanks to the armed struggles of local residents in the mid 19th century, when the nascent Italian state was attempting to incorporate all forests into the national *demanio*. Such struggles took place all over Italy, but only in the north were they so serious and prolonged as to convince the government to create special exceptions in the national law.

An example of community forestry that still exists today thanks to such legal exception is the Magnifica Comunità di Fiemme. In the Magnifica Comunità the forest-managing institutions are strong, maintain a spirit of mutual assistance and solidarity, and provide an important cultural basis for the use of the forest resources. Legally, the forest is owned by "all people of the Fiemme Valley" who comprise the "*vicini*" of 11 townships (a *vicino* is a person who has been living in the valley for 20 years at least, or who is a descendant of a *vicino*). Community forests are inalienable, indivisible and collectively owned and managed. Traditionally, wood was distributed according to the citizen's need to build a house (once in a lifetime) and for maintenance work and heating (once a year). Today, the financial income from the sale of timber is used to support community needs. If in the past those needs were related to road building or health care, today they mostly comprise socio-cultural activities and incentives for people to remain in rural areas. The sawmill industries currently exploiting the collectively-owned forest resources are among the best performing in the whole country, for quality and income. And the forest resources are excellently and sustainably managed.

Another example is the Regole d'Ampezzo of the Ampezzo Valley (where the famous Cortina resort is located), which has a recorded history of approximately 1,000 years. The Regole manage the common property resources initially made available by the extensive work of the early Regolieri (pasture creation and maintenance out of the original woods). To date, the Regolieri comprise only the descendants of the early founders of the community and their sons who remain *residents* in the valley, a more stringent requirement than in the case of the Magnifica Comunità di Fiemme. They hold the property under inalienable and indivisible title. Their general assembly takes management decisions after extensive discussion and by a "qualified majority", a procedure more akin to consensus than voting. The decisions and rules (which, incidentally, is the meaning of the word "regole") are carefully crafted to use the resources sustainably and in non-destructive ways. Unlike in the Fiemme Valley, no dividends are shared among the Regolieri and all the income from the natural resources (e.g., from tourism, sale of timber) is re-invested in their management.

Through time, the early inhabitants of the Ampezzo Valley have maintained their rights of occupation and modes of local production thanks to their skills as diplomats (they managed to ensure agreements with the Venetian Republic in 1420 and, later, with the Austrian Emperors). In 1918, the end of the First World War saw the Ampezzo Valley incorporated within the Italian state. From then to the present, the Regole have often had to struggle to maintain their rare autonomous status under special exceptions in the national legislation and regional laws, a feat that depended on a combination of personal skills of the Regolieri and the importance and visibility of the landscape they have managed to conserve. About 15 years ago, the Regole finally received major recognition as the sole and full legal managers of the *Parco Naturale delle Dolomiti d'Ampezzo*. Thus this regional protected area is established on the land and the resources the local community has conserved through the centuries. From an economic point of view, the Regole are today less directly reliant on the natural resources that they manage, although the unique tourism and real estate value of their valley depends on the magnificent landscape they have maintained. It is notable that they have obtained tax-free status from the Italian government, and secured major project funds and subsidies from the European Union, the Italian state and the Veneto regional government.

Box 5.4   The Tagbanwa strive for the recognition and maintenance of a Community Conserved Area in Coron Island (the Philippines)
(adapted from Ferrari and de Vera, 2003)

The Tagbanwa people of the Philippines inhabit a stunningly beautiful limestone island for which they have established stringent use regulations. The forest resources are to be used for domestic purposes only. All the freshwater lakes but one are sacred. Entry to those lakes is strictly forbidden for all except religious and cultural purposes. The only lake accessible for tourism is Lake Kayangan, which has regulations concerning the number of people allowed in, garbage disposal, resource use, etc. Until recently, the Tagbanwa's territorial rights were not legally recognised, leading to encroachment by migrant fishers, tourism operators, politicians seeking land deals and government agencies. This caused several problems, the main one of which was the impoverishment of the marine resources, essential to local livelihoods. In the mid–1980s, however, the islanders organized themselves into the Tagbanwa Foundation of Coron Island (TFCI) and started lobbying to regain management control over their natural resources.

They first applied for a Community Forest Stewardship Agreement (CFSA), which was granted in 1990 over the 7748 hectares of Coron Island and a neighbouring island, Delian, but not over the marine areas. The Tagbanwa continued their struggle and, in 1998, they managed to get a Certificate of Ancestral Domain Claim for 22,284 hectares of land and marine waters. Finally, in 2001, after having produced a high quality map and an Ancestral Land Management Plan, they managed to obtain a Certificate of Ancestral Domain Title (CADT), which grants collective right to land.

Despite their successful management achievements, the Tagnabwa CADT was later reviewed, as the national policies and systems were being restructured. A governmental proposal was then advanced to add Coron Island to the National Integrated Protected Area System. Despite the fact that the government proposes to set in place a co-management system for the island, the Tagbanwas are opposing these moves, as they fear that they would lose control of their natural resources, and those would be less and not better protected. Very importantly for them, they wish to remain "rightholders" – the owners and protectors of their territories – and refuse to be classified as one "stakeholder" among others.

---

areas established by other social actors or the state) to address a variety of interests and concerns, such as:

- to secure a sustainable provision of goods related to livelihoods (e.g. wildlife or water);

- to satisfy religious, identity or cultural needs (e.g. honouring the memories of ancestors or the deities present in sacred sites, guarding burial sites and protecting ritual places from external interference);

- to maintain crucial ecosystem functions (e.g. soil stability or hydrological cycles);

- to protect wildlife populations for ethical reasons;

- to safeguard their own physical security as well as the security of their properties and settlements, possibly in expectation of harsh ecological conditions such as droughts or floods; and

- to derive economic benefits (as for the community territories recently dedicated to eco-tourism).

In this sense, the primary objectives of the relevant community initiatives are more often defined in relation to community needs, well-being, an ethical world view and sustainable use of natural resources than to the protection of biodiversity or wildlife *per se*. Yet, we speak of Community Conserved Areas only when we see examples of *effective* conservation.

Recently, some areas have also been voluntarily subjected to a conservation regime by indigenous and local communities with the explicit intent of securing land tenure, i.e. obtaining legal recognition of their customary rights to the land and gaining assurance from governments that it will be protected and not relinquished to a variety of forms of exploitation.[118] In certain situations a protected area regime can provide such security, and also attract donor funding, support, visibility and/or income from tourism.[119] The community identity and cohesiveness necessary to establish a Community Conserved Area (see Box 5.5) may also mean that they are better placed to get access to education, health, sanitation, etc. And Community Conserved Areas may promote a more just and egalitarian society, as they require joint initiatives among different classes and castes and some degree of transparency and accountability in governance matters. Under favourable conditions, therefore, the economic and non-economic benefits of establishing Community Conserved Areas can be substantial.

An emphasis on community benefits does not imply that biodiversity conservation is not valued by communities, but that biodiversity is placed in the perspective of human well-being and peaceful development. The case of the Alto Fragua-Indiwasi National Park in Colombia (Box 5.2) is an excellent example. In another case in the Ecuadorian Andes, indigenous communities have established use restrictions and management regulations in areas adjacent to San Pablo Lake in order to prevent further deterioration of the lake's environment – a genuine conservation objective and yet fully related to community livelihoods.[120] In parts of India, communities have in recent times declared forests or grasslands as sacred, so as to conserve them in support of their livelihoods.

So communities have many reasons for protecting areas and resources, and the language and concepts they use to convey these objectives may often be different from the objectives that distinguish the IUCN protected area management categories. Nonetheless, it is possible to find Community Conserved Areas that bring about similar results to those aimed at under each of the management objectives specified by the IUCN management categories (see Table 5.1).

The recognition and status of Community Conserved Areas depend on the particular local, national and regional context. In the Horn of Africa, for example, conservation initiatives conceived and implemented by local communities through their own exclusive means are relatively common. These initiatives are culture-based and culture-specific as they relate in complex ways to the ethnic identity of a community, including

---

[118] See the case of Indigenous Protected Areas in Australia (Box 5.1) and the one of co-management in Bolivia (Box 4.3).

[119] Jones (2003) reports that some community conservancies in Namibia manage several million hectares of land with large animal populations and important habitats, some of which have been set aside as core wildlife and tourism areas. The Torra Conservancy has one up-market tourism lodge generating approx. US$50,000 annually. Trophy hunting is worth nearly US$18,000 annually and a sale of springbok in 2002 raised US$13,000.

[120] Oviedo, 2002.

Box 5.5   Restoring a Community Conserved Area of nomadic pastoralists – livelihoods, nature conservation and cultural identity
(adapted from Borrini-Feyerabend *et al.* 2004, in press)

The Kuhi – one of about 20 sub-tribes of the Shish Bayli Tribe of the Qashqai nomadic pastoralists of southern Iran – have been engaged for a few years in participatory action research about their own "sustainable livelihoods" and the conservation of biodiversity in their landscape. Their action-research is focused on a resource management unit comprising their summering and wintering grounds and their associated migration routes in between. The Kuhi held several workshops and one of the major problems they identified has been the breakdown of the traditional strength of the sub-tribes. They analysed their situation in some depth and decided to recreate their autonomous organization in a manner that would also be able to respond to modern challenges, including notions of participatory democracy. Extended negotiations among them led to the "Council for Sustainable Livelihoods of the Kuhi Migratory Pastoralists" and its associated Community Investment Fund, which is now pursuing initiatives in each of the five categories of problems/needs identified by the sub-tribe. The new idea that excited them the most, however, is about restoring natural resources to their common property care and control.

A unique opportunity in this sense is the Chartang-Kushkizar wetland, extending some 9km in length, shared between the Kuhi and the Kolahli Sub-tribes. This has been a community-conserved wetland from time immemorial. The Kuhi know that they obtain many "ecosystem benefits" from this wetland, including water reserves, reeds for handicrafts, fish, medicinal plants, micro-climate control and wildlife. The government had earmarked part of the area in a controversial plan to be divided up among households for agricultural use. The newly constituted Council believes it is better to preserve this area as a *qorukh* or local reserve – equivalent to a *hema* in other parts of the Middle East. It has thus submitted a petition and a proposal to the relevant government authorities to declare the wetland and the surrounding rangelands as a Community Conserved Area with use rights being regulated by the sub-tribe elders. The petition is currently being reviewed by the government and has so far received encouraging support.

In terms of IUCN categories, the overall Community Conserved Area, covering the Kuhi wintering and summering grounds together with the access routes, could be considered as a Category V protected area (i.e., dedicated to landscape protection), with the wetland portion as Category II (i.e., dedicated to ecosystem protection). This initiative is showing how nomadic livelihoods can be reconciled with conservation and how the cultural identity and organization of the relevant indigenous and local communities are necessary prerequisites for their full involvement in conservation.

---

its governance systems, norms, symbolic constructions and rituals.[121] Unfortunately, these practices are rarely recognised and supported by state governments; indeed it has been argued that the policies of a succession of dominant political powers and developers have undermined community-based conservation in the Horn of Africa. Some pockets within broad landscape-based Community Conserved Areas have lately been granted official protected area status, but the recognition in most cases arrived long after the traditional management practices, which had assured their conservation, had already been undermined (see Box 5.6).

In contrast to events in the Horn of Africa, Community Conserved Areas have fared well in South America. In that region, they are making a significant contribution to

---

[121]   Bassi (2003) refers to these CCAs as prime examples of "ethnic conservation".

Box 5.6   The making of unsustainable livelihoods: eroding the Community-Conserved Landscape of the Oromo-Borana (Ethiopia)
(adapted from Tache, 2000; Tache and Bassi, 2002)

The whole ethnic territory of the Borana, in Ethiopia, can be considered a Community Conserved Area. The territory has been managed for centuries through rules that assured the sustainable use of renewable natural resources. Biodiversity conservation and the sound management of natural resources were promoted through inclusion/exclusion rules applying to all pastoral activities and known as *seera marraa bisanii* – "the law of grass and water". The Borana "law of grass" shares the basic principles of most East African pastoral groups. It differentiates between dry season pastures (with permanent water points) and wet season pastures (with good grass, but only accessible during rains), imposing the maximization of use of wet-season pasture whenever possible (during rains), to minimize pressure on the most intensely utilized rangelands served by permanent water points. The "law of water" is peculiar to the Borana: their environment is characterized by numerous well complexes (the *tulaa* wells being the most famous among them). This law is well articulated, regulating in various ways the social and economic investment necessary to develop traditional wells and water points, access and maintenance. Through the normal cycle of well excavation and collapse, over-exploited dry season areas are abandoned and new ones are developed.

The juniper forests found in Borana lands have a special role, which is common to many East African forests used by pastoralists. Being too humid, they are not suitable for permanent pastoral settlement. Some open patches, however, contain excellent pasture and the forest also provides permanent springs. For centuries, such forests have never been permanently inhabited but reserved as dry-season pasture. They were important as a last refuge for grazing in case of drought, a reserve for medical and ritual plants and for their overall symbolic and ecological significance. They were not subject to special management provisions apart from a very strict prohibition on fires, but were an integral and essential part of the survival system of the Borana. Basically, the Borana managed their environment as a community conserved landscape, with detailed zoning and regulations.

Until the 1970s, this environmentally sound management of natural resources on Borana land assured the conservation of a unique biodiversity heritage (including 43 species of mammals, 283 species of birds and many unique plants and habitats), despite the existence for many years of several small towns close to the main forests. However, the Borana environment was then confronted with major land use changes: the government limited movement within the territory and promoted agriculture. The situation deteriorated further after the change of government in 1991, with the political marginalization of the Borana. UN-backed resettlement programmes and other developments meant that more and more outsiders came into the area, diluting the Borana presence and disrupting their traditional land use systems.

In effect the Borana's ethnic territory had been treated as if their common property land was 'no-man's land', to be assigned to whoever claimed it. As customary common property and Community Conserved Areas are not recognised by the Ethiopian government, the Borana have been squeezed into the driest pockets where their grazing land was bound to deteriorate, all the while their last resort forests were exploited for commercial purposes, with no regard to sustainability. Drought during the last decade arrived on top of all these problems and produced devastating effects and acute livestock destitution. The only possible survival strategy for the Borana has been to engage in farming in the remaining least suitable places, further increasing the amount of land put under cultivation and alienated to the pastoral mode of production. As everyone should have known, the traditional land of the Borana is not suitable for agriculture due to both low and irregular rainfall. Now the Borana have joined millions of other pastoralists and agro-pastoralists in Ethiopia who survive more and more often on food donations from abroad. A unique social system, sustainable land management and dependent biodiversity have all been effectively destroyed.

biodiversity conservation. Indeed national governments are using them to bring more national lands under a conservation regime.[122] The TILCEPA regional review of cases from Spanish-speaking South America reports that large protected areas overlap substantially with traditional community lands. Indeed, it is estimated that about 84% of the lands now lying within South America's National Parks are indigenous and community lands, and in many of these areas communities are regaining legal land and management rights. Soon, a very large proportion of existing protected areas of the region may be indigenous or community-managed, totally or partially.[123]

Table 5.1 Examples of Community Conserved Areas relating to each of the IUCN Categories
(adapted from Kothari, 2003)

IUCN Category and Description	Community Conserved Area type	Field examples[124]
Ia. Strict Nature Reserve and **Ib. Wilderness Areas:** Protected area managed mainly for science or wilderness protection.	Sacred/forbidden or otherwise 'no-use' groves, lakes, springs, mountains, islands, etc. with prohibition on uses except in very particular occasions, such as an annual ceremony, once-a-year collective hunting or fishing strictly regulated by the community. A special case here may be the territories of un-contacted peoples (e.g. in the Amazons). The main reasons for the communities to protect the area may be cultural or religious rather than wilderness or science *per se*.	▪ Coron Island, Palawan, Philippines (sacred beaches, marine areas, lakes) (see Box 5.4) ▪ Life Reserve of Awa People, Ecuador ▪ Forole sacred mountain of Northern Kenya ▪ Hundreds of sacred forests and wetlands, India ▪ Mandailing Province, Sumatra, Indonesia (forbidden river stretches) ▪ Intangible Zones of Cuyabeno-Imuya and Tagaeri-Taromenane, Ecuador
II. National Park: Protected area managed mainly for ecosystem protection and recreation.	Protected watershed forests above villages, community declared wildlife sanctuaries, community-enforced protected reefs and no-take fishing zones. The main objective of community protection may be to obtain the sustainable provision of a resource, such as water, fish, or income from tourism.	▪ Tinangol, Sabah, Malaysia (forest catchment) ▪ Isidoro-Secure National Park, Bolivia ▪ Safety forests, Mizoram, India ▪ Alto Fragua-Indiwasi National Park, Colombia (see Box 5.2)
III. Natural Monument: Protected area managed mainly for conservation of specific natural features.	Natural monuments (caves, waterfalls, cliffs, rocks) protected by the local communities for religious, cultural, or other objectives of specific ethnic or local relevance.	▪ Mapu Lahual Network of Indigenous Protected Areas (Coastal Range Temperate Rainforests), Chile ▪ Limestone Caves, Kanger Ghati National Park and elsewhere, India ▪ Sites of ancestor graves, Madagascar
IV. Habitat/Species Management Area: Protected area managed mainly for conservation through management intervention.	Village waterbodies harbouring waterbird nesting colonies or aquatic wildlife, turtle nesting sites, community managed wildlife corridors and riparian vegetation areas. Local management objectives may be related to spiritual or cultural values and other objectives of specific ethnic or local relevance rather than species protection *per se*.	▪ Pulmarí Protected Indigenous Territory, Argentina (proposed) ▪ Kokkare Bellur, India (heronry) ▪ Sacred crocodile ponds throughout West Africa

---

[122] See, for instance, Luque, 2003.

[123] Oviedo, 2002.

[124] The inclusion of a Community Conserved Area in this table does not indicate that it will necessarily be recognised as a protected area, but that it may achieve a similar outcome and can be equally valuable to conservation.

Table 5.1   Examples of Community Conserved Areas relating to each of the IUCN Categories (cont.)

V. Protected Landscape/Seascape: Protected area managed mainly for landscape/ seascape conservation and recreation.	Traditional grounds of pastoral communities/mobile peoples, including rangelands, water points and forest patches; sacred and cultural landscapes and seascapes; collectively managed river basins; (such natural and cultural ecosystems have multiple land/water uses integrated into each other, and given a context by the overall sacred/ cultural/ productive nature of the ecosystem; they include areas with high agricultural biodiversity among crops and livestock).	▪ Migration territory of the Kuhi nomadic tribe (Iran), including the Chartang-Kushkizar community protected wetland (see Box 5.5) ▪ Palian river basin, Trang Province, Thailand (rainforest, coast, mangroves) ▪ Thateng District, Sekong Province, Laos (agriculture and forestry mosaic) ▪ Potato Park, Peru (see Box 5.7) ▪ Island of Eigg (United Kingdom) ▪ Natural Park of Dolomiti d'Ampezzo, Italy (see Box 5.3) ▪ Coron island, the Philippines (see Box 5.4) ▪ (ancient) Borana territory, Oromo Region, Ethiopia (pastoral territory, with protected savannah, forest, and volcanic areas of Category Ib and III) (see Box 5.6)
VI. Managed Resource Protected Area: Protected area managed mainly for the sustainable use of natural ecosystems.	Resource reserves (forests, grasslands, waterways, coastal and marine stretches, including wildlife habitats) under restricted use and communal rules that assure sustainable harvesting through time.	▪ Community forests in the Val di Fiemme, Italy (see Box 5.3). ▪ Takietà forest, Niger ▪ Pathoumphone District, Champassak Province, Laos (NTFP-based) ▪ Pred Nai, Thailand (mangrove regeneration) ▪ Amarakaeri Communal Reserve, Peru ▪ Kinna, Kenya (bordering Meru National Park; use of medicinal plants) ▪ Jardhargaon, Mendha-Lekha, Arvari, and 100s of others, India (fodder, fuel, water, NTFP, medicinal plants) (see Boxes 5.12 and 5.13)

Characteristics of Community Conserved Areas

Community Conserved Areas can be analysed in various ways. Apart from the objectives of management (partially reflected in the IUCN management category, and supplemented by livelihood/cultural objectives), key distinguishing features are the following:

▪ Size of the area and/or extent of the resources being protected. The size of area may range from as small as a hectare, as for the sacred Peguche falls in Ecuador, to as large as entire mountains, lakes or valleys, as for Lake Titicaca in Peru/ Bolivia; similarly, resources may range from a single species (such as the painted stork or globally threatened spot-billed pelican whose nesting sites are strictly protected by some villages in India) to broader classes of flora or fauna (such as *Ficus* tree species and groves, also in India).

▪ Intrinsic biodiversity value and naturalness of the area and resources being protected (this is highly variable; for the purpose of the definition of a Community Conserved Area used here, the biodiversity/ecological values should be evident, and protection of this value should be aimed at or achieved).

▪ Length of time the protection effort or practice has been sustained (was the area established in the distant past or is it a more recent phenomenon? Was conservation enforced regularly or sporadically?).

▪ Length of time the initiative is likely to be sustained in the future (are impending changes likely to affect the Community Conserved Area? Are there serious threats?).

▪ History, including especially the occasion for establishing the Community Conserved Area (did the area originate through internal or external initiative? Was it a response to a crisis, a threat or a severe shortage in resources? Have the particular time and occasion vanished from memory yet the practice remains a part of local culture and mores? Or has the area emerged as part of a process of local empowerment, regaining rights of self-rule, including control over natural resources?).

▪ Extent of community support (is the Community Conserved Area valued as an essential component of community identity and culture? Is it crucial for the livelihoods of people? Has the community demonstrated a strong will to preserve it, and resilience in facing change that could potentially alter it?).

▪ Effectiveness, legitimacy and embedded equity of its management structure (are all interested actors capable of influencing decisions? Are decisions being implemented and respected? Are decisions generally meaningful and productive? Is transparency upheld as a crucial management characteristic? Are benefits and costs being equitably distributed?).

▪ Ecological performance (is the Community Conserved Area effective in protecting biodiversity and critical ecological services?).

▪ Social and economic performance (is the Community Conserved Area effective in meeting the various needs and aspirations of the community?).

The characteristics above are important as they could make a difference for the survival of Community Conserved Areas in many countries, for instance by determining the level of recognition and support the state and other social actors may be willing to grant it. State recognition and support can also be used to classify Community Conserved Areas, for instance through:

▪ Extent of legal backing and government support (is the area recognised in statutory law or recognised only customarily? Is it supported by governmental agencies?).

▪ Tenure security (does the community have legal ownership and/or control over the area and its resources? Is the Community Conserved Area facing external threats, for instance by private operators?).

▪ Availability of technical support (is the area supported by governmental or non-governmental organizations or other agencies that can facilitate participatory research or provide needed management resources, training, etc.?).

As in the case of Co-managed Protected Areas, various combinations of characteristics have been used to distinguish between "strong" and "weak" Community Conserved Areas. For instance, the regional review commissioned by TILCEPA in South-East Asia[125] analyses a series of cases ranging from weak Community Conserved Areas (an externally-originated, community-based initiative in Myanmar/Burma, which secured only temporary tenure rights through a 25 year lease) to strong Community Conserved Areas (an internally-originated initiative to protect an ancestral domain in the Philippines, fully backed by local practice and culture, strongly supported by NGOs, and with the community entitled with ownership rights because of relevant national legislation). Other strong models of this kind have been described in Boxes 5.1, 5.2 and 5.3 (Australia, Colombia and Italy).

Many community initiatives integrate the management of both 'wild' and 'domesticated' species. Some may look at them as part of a continuum, from predominantly wild to semi-wild, semi-domesticated and predominantly domesticated[126] (see Box 5.7). Traditional practices that make best use of the full range of biodiversity include some Indian villages, where farmers are both involved in forest conservation and reviving a range of agro-biodiversity practices, including trials of hundreds of varieties of rice, beans and other crops; they believe that these two practices are closely connected and mutually beneficial.

Many Community Conserved Areas stretch our understanding of the concept of "area", as the territories under protection do not at all times have clear borders, being associated with forces of nature or influenced by the seasons and climatic phenomena. This is particularly true in the case of mobile indigenous peoples, who relate to very broad territories and resources affected by varying climatic conditions. Since time immemorial, mobile indigenous peoples utilised practices, such as *hema*, whereby an area is subtracted from use – and thus actively protected – only for a deter-mined number of months or years. More generally, ethnic conservation[127] – i.e. the conservation practices proper to an ethnic group, based on their unique institutions and cultural norms – does not tend to work through exclusive associations between a given community and a given territory or marine area, but commonly includes over-lapping entitlements, where different communities, tribes and clans have legitimate rights and responsibilities related to different resources, types of uses, timings etc. Several ethnic groups may be concerned about the same territory and their *combined* management practices may be effective for conservation. In other words, a territory or marine area may simultaneously be a Community Conserved Area for more than one community (see Box 5.8).

[125] Ferrari, 2002.

[126] For a fuller account of the relationship between the conservation of agro-biodiversity and Category V protected areas, see Phillips (2002).

[127] Bassi, 2003.

Box 5.7   The Potato Park, Peru
(from a personal communication by Alejandro Argumedo, 2003)

In the highlands of Peru, six communities of the Quechua peoples have established a Potato Park (*Parque de la Papa*) in a unique initiative to conserve domesticated and wild biodiversity. Over 8,500 hectares of titled communal land are being jointly managed to conserve about 1,200 potato varieties (cultivated and wild) as well as the natural ecosystems of the Andes. Since this region is the one of origin of the potato, the effort is of global significance.

The Potato Park was initiated by an indigenous-run organization, the Quechua-Aymara Association for Sustainable Livelihoods-ANDES. The villages entered into an agreement with the International Potato Institute to repatriate 206 additional varieties, and have a long-term goal to re-establish in the valley all of the world's 4,000 known potato varieties. Traditional techniques are being augmented by new ones, including greenhouses, education on potato varieties through video filming in the local language, production of medicines for local sale, and establishment of a database. Native species are being used to regenerate forests, and a form of "agro-ecotourism" is being developed. The initiative has brought together communities that had land conflicts, in part also through the revival of the village boundary festival, in which the boundaries are "walked". The Potato Park is a powerful example of an integrated protected landscape, suitable for IUCN's Category V designation (and is cited as such in IUCN's guidelines on Category V protected areas – Phillips (2002)). Despite this, it has not yet received a formal status in Peru's protected area system.

Some common features of Community Conserved Areas

The following features are common to most Community Conserved Areas:

- They are tied to the community's sense of identity and culture. The establishment of a Community Conserved Area is usually linked to the collective purposes and aspirations of the relevant community, and most Community Conserved Areas are managed as part of a community's ethical norms, cultural features and plans for the future.

- They relate closely to the community's long-term livelihood and land/water management strategies. Protection measures are generally connected to spaces

---

Box 5.8   Forole, the sacred mountain of the Galbo people, Ethiopia
(adapted from Bassi, 2003)

Forole is a sacred mountain just north of the border between Kenya and Ethiopia where the Galbo peoples (a sub-group of the Gabbra) hold the *jila galana* ceremonies. Most of the Galbo live in Kenya, but they move in pilgrimage to the Forole on the occasion of the ceremony. The trees of Forole Mountain are totally protected by the Gabbra and access to the upper part is only allowed to a few people who preside over the ceremony of the sacrifice to the Sacred Python. The lower part of the mountain provides permanent water and is used as reserve grazing area by both the Gabbra and the Borana pastoralists. Sometimes there are tensions over pastoral resources between the two groups, but the Borana fully respect the sacredness of Forole Mountain and the inherent restrictions, indirectly assuring its conservation. This Community Conserved Area is thus not unequivocally associated with a single ethnic group.

---

and activities dedicated to material and cultural production. The high management standards achieved by many communities are a result of the tangible benefits derived from the good management of resources. Because of the connection between Community Conserved Areas and livelihoods, supporting these areas may help to reduce poverty.

- They involve areas and resources under common property, or under private property that are subject to community rules; and they possess relatively simple procedures for administration and decision-making. Community Conserved Areas are sanctioned and managed within community institutions, where community members discuss the benefits, costs and trade-offs of different initiatives and make decisions that gradually become integrated into community norms. Such a direct form of governance, effective as long as the community is culturally cohesive, can be adapted to local circumstances and does not depend so much on external factors.

- They safeguard many structural and functional features of ecosystems and the landscape. The segregation of areas for protection within traditional lands is normally not based on valuation of biodiversity "exceptions" and uniqueness (endemism, rare species, etc.) but on cultural values that reflect complex ecological processes (species migrations, reproduction areas, genetic flows via corridors, etc.), many of which go beyond the border of the specific Community Conserved Area. Protection is provided to wide strips of forests, zones of water recharge, migratory routes and the like, thereby offering wide and effective safeguards for the continuation of long-term evolutionary processes.[128]

- They maintain costs (especially financial) at relatively low levels. Costs of maintaining Community Conserved Areas are normally largely covered by the economic activities of the communities themselves and by their various existing systems and structures. These costs, and especially those of surveillance and protection, are low compared to the costs of official, state-managed protected areas of comparable size that need to employ salaried staff. The opportunity costs of Community Conserved Areas – such as land taken out of production and volunteer labour – can be significant, however, and material and non-material benefits need to be achieved to justify the social investments.

Options for action and advice

As staff of national or local protected area agencies, authorities at various levels, relevant NGOs and community leaders become aware of the existence and conservation value of Community Conserved Areas, they may wish to see their profile raised and support to them increased. What options do they have, and what advice do they need? Within the context of the broad policy options reviewed in Chapter 6, some actions can be of crucial help. Ideally, protected area agencies and organizations should begin by undertaking a comprehensive programme to inventory, map, study and support all Community Conserved Areas in the region or country. This work, however, can also be undertaken

---

[128] Oviedo, 2002.

for smaller geographical units, or for a sample only of all the Community Conserved Areas. Close study of, and support for, a single Community Conserved Area can be a useful first step for an organization wishing to learn about this form of conservation, leading to a fuller programme of co-operation with many more such areas in future. Readers concerned with an individual Community Conserved Area or a number of existing and/or potential such areas at the landscape level are invited to review the menu of options provided below, and to select and adapt those options that best fit their circumstances.

5.1 Gain a broad initial understanding of the relevant Community Conserved Areas

Given the relatively recent introduction of Community Conserved Areas into formal conservation thinking (indeed, in many countries, the concept has yet to arrive), available background information is likely to be scattered and scarce. So the best way to begin may be to collect the basic information needed for a broad initial understanding of what Community Conserved Areas exist. Even in the case of a single Community Conserved Area, it is always advisable to investigate the landscape/seascape to which it belongs and find out whether the case in point is unique or fits a general pattern.

5.1.1 Carry out an initial inventory and mapping of the Community Conserved Areas

An initial inventory of Community Conserved Areas can be based on information collected from various sources, including communities themselves (their elders in particular), but also representatives from various local ethnic groups, government officials, and anthropologists, historians, conservationists and environmental scientists. At this stage, it is helpful to adopt a broad understanding of what a "community conserved area" may be and list all possible cases encountered in the landscape/seascape. This list will contain mostly specific places but should also note relevant features in the landscape (e.g., ancient subterranean water channels), relevant stories and names (e.g., considering that a given species is a bearer of luck) or the persistence of relevant rules and practices (e.g., the fruits of a certain type of tree are considered common property in the region and not commercialized). A preliminarily list might even contain a number of places where it is not immediately apparent that conservation is in fact taking place, nor how much control the community has. It is likely that – within a particular landscape or seascape – a number of possible Community Conserved Areas will be identified in various "states of health", some still vibrant and alive, others jeopardised or in the process of fading away, and still others existing only in local memory or other form of record.

Information for the Community Conserved Areas inventory can be gathered through a call to the public, using as far as possible local languages and different media, and drawing on various documents, such as anthropological and historical accounts of local communities, forestry or fisheries records, gazettes and records kept by various authorities in national and sub-national archives. Natural resource management initiatives that do not explicitly or primarily deal with conservation, such as participatory forestry or fisheries, may also contain valuable examples of Community Conserved Areas. In India and Nepal, for instance, community forestry initiatives at a number of sites have become excellent forest habitats with considerable conservation value, voluntarily managed by the local communities.

Even more important than lists and inventories are maps depicting the location (and other data) of Community Conserved Areas. These could be compiled at the landscape level or for a given Community Conserved Area: in either case the exercise should be done by and/or with the relevant communities.

5.1.2 Identify the key communities and community representatives managing the Community Conserved Areas

A human community is always central to any Community Conserved Area initiative. This may appear obvious but merits re-statement since some case studies of Community Conserved Areas have listed names of sites and ecological information but little or no information on the relevant communities.[129] Thus, even at the initial stage of gathering information, it is crucial to identify the communities managing the Community Conserved Areas, and the key institutions that may exist for the purpose. Ideally, the contact details of one or more individuals who may act as contact points for each area should also be identified.[130]

5.1.3 Trace the historical context of the Community Conserved Areas

Most countries and regions have a history of land and water use by indigenous peoples and/or local communities. A considerable part of this history may not be documented, or may only be represented by biased accounts produced in colonial or modern state times. Nevertheless, what does exist may provide useful information on Community Conserved Areas and illuminate the historical context within which these existed. This would include accounts of traditional and customary systems of land/water management and the relationship of such systems with rulers and state institutions, indigenous knowledge systems, etc. Rather than an in-depth understanding of the history of any particular site or Community Conserved Area of concern, at the initial stage it would be best to compile information about the broad historical context within which Community Conserved Areas should be understood.

5.1.4 Assess the bio-geographic and bio-cultural coverage of Community Conserved Areas

An initial Community Conserved Areas inventory and mapping exercise can be super-imposed on bio-geographic and socio-cultural maps (e.g. maps reporting the distribution of different ethnic and cultural groups, including their territories, resources and routes of mobility) at the level of the relevant landscape. This provides a rough idea of the ecological and social coverage provided by Community Conserved Areas, of possible linkages with official protected areas and other natural resource bodies, and of key gaps.

---

[129] As revealed in many of the case studies received in the current compilation of a directory of Community Conserved Areas in India (Pathak *et al.*, 2004).

[130] These persons may not necessarily represent the entire community nor provide a full understanding of the community conservation initiative, so it is important to consider them only as initial points of contact.

5.2 Support community-led studies and demarcation of the relevant Community Conserved Areas

After gaining an initial understanding of any Community Conserved Areas in the landscape/seascape of concern, the protected area agencies, authorities, NGOs and other leaders may wish to enter into direct contact with the communities concerned. At the request of the communities – and always with their informed consent – they could do so by supporting studies and assessments. These should be carried out by the relevant communities on their own, or with outside agencies.

5.2.1 Support community-led in depth assessments of Community Conserved Areas

Community-led studies are needed for each Community Conserved Area, to provide greater depth to the information in the initial broad inventories (Section 5.1). The studies may cover the various characteristics described above as well as additional ones and others more specific, such as the ones listed in 5.11.

In collecting data of this kind, the community should itself be free to decide whether to request or accept technical, financial or technological inputs (e.g. GIS tools and cartographic equipment, see Box 5.13). The results of such assessments can be used in many ways, such as to improve the community's own understanding of the environment, to identify new resources and ways to use them sustainably or to reinforce existing management practices that have been shown to help conserve biodiversity (see Box 5.9). The scale of such work can be considerable: in Canada for example, the Nunavut atlas contains 27 community maps covering land use and wildlife descriptions for 58 regions; similar land use and ecological knowledge databases have been established by the Inuit in Labrador combined with information on environmental impact assessments.[131] By working with scientists and other governmental or NGO staff, the community may be able to develop indicators to help them to "build up their case".

Finally it should be stressed that, as part of the study and through mapping exercises, the community will have to confirm or re-define their understanding of the land and resources that belong to the Community Conserved Area. This is likely to strengthen the community's sense of relationship with it, and clarify its collective vision for the area's future.

5.2.2 Support the demarcation of the territories and resources of indigenous peoples and local and mobile communities.

In traditional land tenure, permanent physical boundaries are often less important than resource boundaries, which are changing and adaptable. Under modern legal systems, however, the recognition of land rights requires the identification of permanent physical boundaries. This is the process known as demarcation, which involves not only the physical identification and signalling of borders, but a complex process of recognition and mapping of a territory, often carried out together with a biodiversity inventory.

Either as a precondition for the legal recognition of ownership and access rights, or as a provisional alternative to it, demarcation is a central requirement for tenure security of

---

[131] Larsen, 2000.

Checklist 5.1   Features to be covered in community-led in-depth assessments of Community Conserved Areas (CCAs)

- The ecological and biological features, including habitat and species inventories, and trends in ecological status.

- The natural resources in the area and an analysis of the ecological impacts of resource use and other human activities.

- The social and economic features of the area, including its historical development,[132] socio-cultural resources and socio-cultural relevance, current entitlements (both private and collective,[133]) economic benefits and costs, and equity issues.

- The objectives for which the area is managed.

- As appropriate, the relevant IUCN management category to which the CCA could in theory be assigned.

- The body of customary and modern laws and rules that communities have evolved to govern the area,[134] and the extent to which such laws and rules are known and respected within and outside the community of concern.

- The key local actors and organizations that manage the area, including an analysis of their current vitality and effectiveness.

- The differential rights and responsibilities assigned to different groups within the community, in particular regarding socially disadvantaged groups such as women, ethnic and religious minorities, the landless and mobile peoples.

- The history of relationship between the community and official agencies, including how conflicts have been identified and dealt with.[135]

- The extent to which the community management practices manage to maintain ecological values and address socio-cultural and economic needs.

- A threat assessment for the CCA, noting threats from both within and outside the community, including to the sustainability of their management practices.

- An identification of conservation needs and opportunities, including needs to protect and restore ecosystems, and of the community's collective vision for the future of the area.

- Extent and form of internal and external recognition and support given to the CCA, and by whom; and an assessment of the importance of such recognition and support.

---

[132] Here the community's own oral historical knowledge should be collected together with any documentary sources.

[133] The distinction between common and private property is often blurred, depending on specific resources, seasons and practices. An area may be common property for grazing, but its trees may be under private property. See the illuminating example provided by Baird and Dearden, 2003.

[134] This includes identifying indigenous territories and ancestral domains, and any treaties or long-standing agreements relating to these.

[135] For instance, have land reforms or official land ownership patterns taken *common property* ownership into account or has emphasis been on individual land titling only?

Box 5.9   Indigenous management revitalized for a coastal area in Cuvu Tikina (Fiji Islands)

(from Hugh Govan, personal communication, 2003)

The South Pacific Islanders relate with their coastal resources through a vast body of traditional ecological knowledge and management systems. In the second half of the 20th century the state of these coastal resources greatly deteriorated in parallel with the erosion of traditional management of these areas. Fortunately, in recent years there has been a revitalization of indigenous coastal management practices around the Pacific, for example in Vanuatu, Fiji and Western Samoa.

In Cuvu Tikina (Fiji), the communities and a local NGO worked together to map and evaluate the natural resources, to generate and exchange information and to plan together. Besides local management plans, the communities agreed to establish closed fishing areas, to set up an environment committee and to hire fish wardens (trained and supported by the Fisheries Department) to take care of day to day management. The closed fishing areas are based on the traditional system of "taboo" in which areas or species can be restricted for differing lengths of time. These systems were reviewed and re-appreciated as part of the planning process. Results so far are very encouraging and include the recovery of some species' populations and the strengthening of relations between the community and various regional and governmental institutions and tourist operators.

---

indigenous and local communities. It also provides the basis for the legal recognition of community territories and Community Conserved Areas in particular. In recent years, in the Amazon region and elsewhere, there has been a strong engagement in the demarcation of collective territories, in many cases carried out by indigenous peoples with the support of external organizations.[136]

As part of the demarcation exercise, communities often identify areas where they would like to see protection measures established and make decisions about strengthening or creating their Community Conserved Areas.[137] Once demarcation is done, steps need to be taken for its legal recognition, particularly for areas identified for special conservation purposes. This is most important where local communities, and areas that they conserve, are in danger from conflicts over lands and resources, and where external forces may resort to violence, abuse and encroachment into community lands. Effective protection of community territorial boundaries could start with awareness-raising campaigns directed to the general public but also to government agencies and decision-makers, whose "development plans" may pose serious threats to community territories.[138]

5.2.3   Support the participatory monitoring and evaluation of Community Conserved Area initiatives

Communities often have their own ways of assessing the success or failure of their Community Conserved Area. They ask questions like "Has fuel/fodder/fish output

---

[136]   See for example Plant and Hvalkof, 2001. Simeón Jiménez, an indigenous Yekuana from Venezuela, concludes from his experience that, for biodiversity and cultural conservation, demarcation comes first. The Yekuana Nonodü self-demarcated their territory in the mid-90s (Gonzalez and Arce, 2001).

[137]   The San Miguel-Bermejo Ecological Reserve of the Cofan people in Ecuador is a good example (Oviedo, 2002).

[138]   Those campaigns that cannot be run by the communities themselves and should be the responsibility of government agencies and supporting organizations.

increased?"; "Has the forest cover increased?"; "Have water sources become more reliable?"; "Have populations of target species increased?"; or "Have the local people gained more secure livelihoods?" The indicators they use will depend on the objectives for which the area is being managed and the extent of community knowledge. Useful inputs can be made by outside agencies through the introduction of additional indicators, the advice of non local experts, training on new methods and tools (e.g. GPS/GIS/ computers) to generate information, and an overall independent, fresh input into the monitoring and evaluation process. Some relevant questions to explore are listed in Checklist 5.2.

5.3 Support communities' efforts to have Community Conserved Areas legally recognised and, if appropriate and communities so desire, incorporated into official protected area systems

Many communities that manage Community Conserved Areas lack legal support for their initiatives. Most Community Conserved Areas are not recognised as a protected entity under statutory law, and few existing legal frameworks are able to accommodate collective and customary rights and responsibilities in natural resource management. This makes it much easier for outsiders (and for some community members) to violate the norms laid down by the community. Lack of legal recognition can also be a hindrance to gaining wider social recognition and the financial, administrative, or political support that Community Conserved Areas need. Policy reforms that may encourage support for community-based conservation include the integration of Community Conserved Areas into national protected area systems through new legislation, new interpretations of existing legislation, the establishment of new or reformed protected area institutions designed to work more closely with communities, and the adoption of new agency policies with similar aims. The suggested steps below address agencies, NGOs and community leaders working to assist Community Conserved Areas within an existing policy milieu, while Chapter 6 sets out a fuller discussion of the development of an appropriate legislative and policy framework for Community Conserved Areas.

5.3.1 Upon community request, assist communities in gaining official recognition of the conservation value of individual Community Conserved Areas

In some cases, Community Conserved Areas have significant conservation value, but it may not be suitable to incorporate them into the national or sub-national protected area system for a variety of reasons. However, they may still acquire legal recognition in other ways. For example, it may be possible to designate them as 'biodiversity heritage sites', 'conservation sites' or give some other kind of national or local protection, perhaps under biodiversity legislation.[139] Additionally, participatory forestry laws in some countries make provisions for legal backing of community managed sites. And laws relating to decentralization can also provide space for recognition of Community Conserved Areas, or could so be interpreted with suitable guidelines. Other agreements or contractual

---

[139] Note that the CBD specifically allows for this, since Article 8(a) raises the importance of areas other than protected areas, "where special measures need to be taken to conserve biodiversity" (see also Box 5.12).

Checklist 5.2   Questions to explore in participatory monitoring and evaluation of Community Conserved Areas (CCAs)

- Is the community fully in control of governance and management of the CCA? Does it possess all the necessary capacities?

- Is the CCA, as currently governed and managed by the community, likely to be sustained in the long run in financial, institutional and social terms?

- Is the CCA well-managed? Is it helping to conserve ecosystems, species and environmental services?

- Is the CCA improving the community's social, economic, and political situation?

- Are the cultural, intellectual, and other values and skills of the community being protected and enhanced because of the CCA?

- Are the less privileged sectors of the community adequately involved in decision making about the CCA and benefiting from it? Are inequities being reduced?

arrangements for the management of Community Conserved Areas could be in the form of long-term leases or conservation easements, incorporating the recognition of mutual obligations between the state and the community. In all such cases, the indigenous peoples and local and mobile communities should be able to "demonstrate" to the relevant authorities the conservation value of the site and its resources, and be clear as to what results they would like to obtain from official recognition.

5.3.2   Upon community request, assist communities in obtaining the incorporation of Community Conserved Areas into the national or sub-national protected area systems

The legal recognition of Community Conserved Areas as part of the national protected area system could provide them with the same status as government-established protected areas, and would be suitable where such areas meet the definition and the criteria of a protected area under national legislation and policy; or it could be used to recognise them as separate, complementary conservation initiatives. In all cases, it is imperative that the form of legal recognition is appropriate to the context and that it safeguards the right of communities to retain or develop their own governance and management arrangements rather than forcing them to follow a single national model.

It may be tempting for conservation authorities to declare Community Conserved Areas on their own. This could be counter-productive, however, as it may go against the process by which communities become comfortable with all that is entailed in gaining legal recognition and, possibly, see their area as part of the conservation system. Therefore legal recognition of a Community Conserved Area should be pursued only at the request of the concerned community, and with its prior informed consent.

Providing legal recognition to an individual Community Conserved Area as part of a national protected area system could proceed according to the steps outlined in Checklist 5.3.

Box 5.10   Wirikuta, the Huichol Sacred Space in the Chihuahuan Desert of San Luis Potosi, Mexico, becomes a government-recognised Sacred Natural Site

(adapted from Otegui, 2003)

The Wirikuta sacred land of the Huichol people is located in the state of San Luis Potosi of Mexico, expanding through the municipalities of Catorce, Matehuala, Villa de Paz and Villa Guadalupe. "Wirikuta" comes from the Huichol word *wirima*, which means to anoint or to touch, for the Huichols consider that different deities and ancestors that dwell in this sacred place touch them magically.

This sacred land is a traditional pilgrimage route, which the Huichol people have used and preserved for centuries. However, most of the land within the route lies outside legal Huichol lands. This was for a long time a reason for concern to the Huichol, as they had no legal or political power to influence management of the areas outside their lands. After a lengthy process of negotiating with the state government and stakeholders, Wirikuta was finally decreed as a Sacred Natural Site in June 2001 by the government of the state of San Luis Potosi. It currently belongs to the San Luis Potosi Network of Protected Areas, made up of a total of 19 protected areas.

A particularly challenging situation is presented by Community Conserved Areas that lie within existing government-designated protected areas but where there is no formal recognition of the communities' ties to them and/or the management history and current practices. Such areas might still be managed by communities – or the community may no longer do so but still feel that the area is important and strongly related to them. Support to communities wishing to gain recognition of Community Conserved Areas that are now within designated protected areas requires exploration of both the state's and the communities' claims and concerns. National protected area agencies may be amenable to recognising community claims if they can, at the same time, retain significant conservation guarantees. In short, the partnership between state and community in such cases is likely to be strongest when both rights and responsibilities are recognised (see Box 5.11).

5.3.3   Upon community request, assist communities in gaining international recognition of Community Conserved Areas

The recognition of Community Conserved Areas as valid entities for conservation by the CBD[140] has opened up the possibility of their inclusion in relevant international systems. In cases where these areas are also protected areas, communities can be helped to give these areas international standing by:

- Nominating them for inclusion in the World Database of Protected Areas;

- Nominating them for inclusion in the United Nations List of Protected Areas (this would normally be done through a national protected area agency);

- Providing information on Community Conserved Areas for inclusion in any future reporting on the state of world's protected areas (e.g. to future World Parks Congresses);

---

[140]   As set out in the CBD Programme of Work on Protected Areas, 2004.

Checklist 5.3   Steps towards gaining recognition of individual Community Conserved Areas (CCAs) within the national or sub-national protected area system

- Determine whether a CCA and its current governance system fit within the protected area definition and/or criteria under national legislation and policy, as well as under IUCN and CBD definitions for the purposes of international registries and classification.

- If so, determine whether it fits within the existing protected area categories of the country concerned. Could the CCA qualify as a national park, sanctuary, game reserve, or other existing PA category? Importantly, would such a category allow for the community's own governance system to continue? Would it allow for management objectives that may be conceptually and/or practically different from conservation *per se*?

- When national legislation and policies are fully compatible with local practice, conservation agencies should grant, or formally recognise, that authority and decision-making powers for the management of the CCA should rest with local communities. Importantly, this will enable them to enforce their decisions (as in the case in which an ordinance for the control of fishing may provide the needed legal backing to a community-declared marine sanctuary).

- When there is incompatibility between community management and national protected area categories, legal and policy adjustments will be required to the current statutory provisions so that the relevant community can retain its governance system. Often, what the communities request is a guarantee of customary tenure, use and access rights, usually sanctioned through a demarcation of territories and resources. For that to happen, however, it may be necessary that the community institution in charge of the management of the CCA be recognised as a legal persona. This may result in changes in the ways a community organizes itself and manages the area. It is important that the community itself determines such matters.

- After the incompatibility is removed, the agency should embark on a process of negotiation, which may end in a contractual arrangement between the community concerned and the national or sub-national conservation authorities. This contractual arrangement may recognise the CCA and provide to it some form of legal protection or support. In other cases, it may transform the area into a *de facto* Co-managed Protected Area.

- Once agreement has been reached between the community and the protected area agency about recognising the CCA as a protected area, jointly agreed rules and regulations are needed for managing it. These may simply involve recording the community's existing rules, without interference from the state agencies, or incorporating new advice, methods and tools. The rules should specify what kind of land and resource zoning exist, what community and individual rights (including ownership) exist, what institutional structures manage the area, whether and how sustainable resource harvesting is allowed to take place (e.g. with limits on quantity, species and seasons). It may also be useful to clarify and record the subdivision of rights and responsibilities within the community itself and to specify provisions against the misuse of rights and power on the part of both the community and government authorities.

- Clarify how the CCA boundaries are to be effectively enforced and protected against external threats. What kind of community-based surveillance and enforcement mechanisms are recognised by the state? For instance, can community members apprehend violators? Who judges in the event of controversies? Who is responsible for the information campaigns needed for the general public to respect CCAs?

> **Box 5.11   Community Conserved Areas as systems of community-based rights and responsibilities**
>
> Land and resource **rights** are fundamental to the socio-cultural and economic life of indigenous peoples and local and mobile communities. They provide them some measure of control over their own destinies and make worthwhile their investment in those long-term activities that are needed for conservation and sustainable resource use. Different communities claim different sets of rights to land and natural resources. Indigenous peoples may view Community Conserved Areas as part of a broader bundle of territorial rights connected to self-determination, while other communities may be more specifically concerned with accessing and using natural resources.
>
> Most traditional rights are accompanied by corresponding **responsibilities** towards nature, natural resources and fellow humans. Throughout all forms of possible legal recognition of Community Conserved Areas it is crucial that this dual approach to rights and responsibilities is maintained, guarding against the possible misuse of rights to alienate or destroy natural resources, or conversely, ensuring that responsibilities are not assigned without the necessary rights and powers to enable their fulfilment. One of the major lessons learned in the last decades of field-based conservation is that management improves when the rights and responsibilities are assigned in a fair and balanced way to each of the parties to an agreement.

- Providing case studies and information on Community Conserved Areas to the CBD Secretariat for dissemination and discussion in CBD meetings and events.

5.4   Provide various forms of support to Community Conserved Areas in an empowering and capacity building mode

Indigenous and local communities and their organizations may require new and rather sophisticated capacities and resources in order to interact effectively with government agencies and conservation NGOs in a formal setting.[141] And, when they are fully accepted as co-managers or managers, they face new roles and responsibilities for which they may not be entirely prepared. Assistance to local institutions to gain legal recognition is one means of supporting Community Conserved Areas, but financial, technical, institutional or security-related support may also be warranted. What is crucial, however, is that these inputs are provided upon the request, or with the prior informed consent, of the communities concerned, and based on a good understanding of the local situation. In some exceptional situations there may be a case for external inputs or interventions, such as when a Community Conserved Area faces an imminent threat from an external or internal agent, but these should rarely happen, be based on the best available knowledge, and always be undertaken in the interests only of conservation and the community.

5.4.1   Build the capacity of communities according to their identified interests and needs

Some of the new capacities needed for communities seeking official recognition for their Community Conserved Area, whether it be inside or outside a formal protected area system, include:

---

[141]   And government agencies (policy makers and on-the-ground staff) benefit from training and support in order to work effectively with indigenous and local communities. These needs will be addressed in Chapter 6.

- The capacity to assess various aspects of their conserved areas and resources (e.g. the boundaries, flora and fauna inventories, socio-economic and cultural importance) through the use of conventional data collection methods or more innovative and participatory methods, such as community resource assessment and mapping.

- The capacity to clarify the community's own interests and concerns regarding the Community Conserved Area.

- The capacity to involve different sectors of the community, such as youth, women, different lineages and clans, in the consultative and decision-making process.

- The capacity to interact effectively with external groups such as other communities, industry, NGOs and government agencies.

- The capacity to participate in regional and national discussions and hearings on protected area management.

- The capacity to manage institutions and finances, both internally and externally derived.

- The capacity to handle appropriate technologies.

Many communities and their organizations will also benefit from acquiring problem analysis and solution-building techniques, which may also require literacy, numeracy and basic management skills. Since increased rights and responsibilities for natural resource management affect the decision-making mechanisms within or between communities, it is crucial to strengthen the community's capacity to develop and apply effective and equitable local institutions, i.e. organizations and associated rules. A step-wise approach to capacity building is recommended for the governmental agencies, authorities, NGOs and leaders willing to assist in the process (see Checklist 5.4).

5.4.2 Assist communities in gaining social recognition

Community initiatives in natural resource management have been historically devalued, not least by some conservation policies and agencies. Fortunately, a reversal of this attitude is underway in many countries, which is a welcome step towards strengthening Community Conserved Areas. Recognition of the value of community-based conservation can be promoted in many ways, e.g. through media coverage, national or international awards (see Box 5.12 below) and invitations to community members to address gatherings and conferences and contribute to training initiatives.

As far as possible, the whole community should be involved and recognised, not just individuals from within it. The media has a tendency to focus on specific individuals, portraying them as the 'heroes' in the story. The achievements of exceptional individuals should not be ignored, but these usually depend on some kind of collective community effort, which should also be recognised. Naturally, when one or more individuals have achieved conservation *despite* a hostile local environment, the recognition of their exceptional achievements is fully justified.

An effective way to raise the profile is through the promotion and support of links among Community Conserved Areas, and between such areas and government and private protected areas. This may strengthen both the conservation outcome (e.g. because of enhanced biological connectivity) and the social knowledge and status of the conservation initiatives.

5.4.3 Assist communities in gaining economic and financial support

Communities often lack the economic means to manage their Community Conserved Areas. However, it may be possible to generate the required support, for example through the measures listed in Checklist 5.5. Such measures may be developed by negotiation between the communities themselves, public agencies and/or private sponsors.

Caution is always advisable in the case of financial support. Many communities in economically poorer parts of the world do not have the capacity to handle large sums of money. If the funds are managed by one or a few individuals within the community, it

---

Checklist 5.4   Steps to strengthen community capacities and have their Community Conserved Areas officially recognised

- *Assess the feasibility of putting new capacities into practice and elicit the community's felt needs*. Several issues are crucial here. Are the necessary human and financial resources available within the community and from external agencies? Is the policy environment supportive of community institutions playing their roles or is there a risk of raising false expectations? Is the community prepared to take on new capacities? Are there socio-cultural impacts to be expected as new capacities are acquired? Have capacity building needs been identified by communities and local organizations themselves or only by external partners?

- *Provide capacity-building initiatives as soon as possible*. Capacity building activities can begin as soon as an agreement to work together has been reached between communities and the protected area agencies. At the beginning, key community representatives may be asked to join information seminars and some training sessions. Over time, community capacities should be strengthened in a structured and sequential manner, involving as many local actors as possible.

- *Have clear and transparent criteria about who should be involved*. Relations within and between communities should be taken into account in choosing whom to involve in capacity building, as this may lead to struggles for influence within communities. To avoid this, clear and transparent selection criteria are important as well as relying on more than one or a few individuals only. The criteria should be elicited from the community itself.

- *Use locally appropriate methods, tailored to the specific situation*. Using locally appropriate language and methods is crucial to effective learning. 'Learning by doing' and visually oriented methodologies are generally much better than lectures. Whereas intensive crash-courses and one-time training sessions can "trigger" new initiatives, communities appear to benefit most from long-term support that is directly relevant to their specific situation.

- *Ensure that capacity building is accompanied by strengthened roles, responsibilities and concrete opportunities* to put new skills into practice. Building capacities without effective avenues of using them may be frustrating for the community.

- *Monitor and evaluate the capacity-building exercise in an on-going way*. Learning processes greatly benefit from self-assessment and evaluation exercises. Feedback can then be used to adjust further initiatives in terms of capacities addressed, participants, methods, etc.

Box 5.12 Bhaonta-Kolyala (Arvari) receives an award from the President of India
(adapted from Shresth and Devidas, 2001; Pathak *et al.*, 2004)

In March 2000, the twin villages of Bhaonta-Kolyala in the arid region of Rajasthan, western India, received an honour that perhaps no other village in India can boast of. The President of India visited their region to bestow on them an award for exemplary work in conservation. The award was well deserved, for the residents of Bhaonta-Kolyala have achieved in 15 years what many government departments could not in decades. Their community organization (Tarun Bharat Sangh) had revived their dying stream Arvari, built decentralized water harvesting structures and protected catchment forests above the structures to minimize siltation. In 1995, a decade after starting the initiative, the villagers had declared 1200 hectares of the regenerating forest as a "public sanctuary", to match the efforts of the government in the nearby Sariska Tiger Reserve, and turned their area from a water-deficient to a water-surplus environment.

Bhaonta-Kolyala's example has been emulated by several dozen villages in the region, resulting in the revival of forests and wildlife in a considerable part of both the tiger reserve and its surrounds. More generally, these initiatives are part of an enormous array of Community Conserved Areas in India. There are perhaps thousands of sacred sites, catchment forests, village wetlands, common pastures, mountain and coastal ecosystems including turtle nesting sites, and other areas that are under the conservation management of local communities. A database of about 300 such sites has recently been prepared, and more and better efforts at documentation would undoubtedly yield many, many more.

---

can strengthen those already in power, or create new power bases with resulting conflicts. Moreover, the funds are also usually handled by men, adding to the disadvantages that women face – however some funding programmes require that finances are handled by women, as this has been more reliable.[142] Financial rewards and compensation are also the easiest means for external agencies to wield power over the community. For these reasons, supporting agencies need to think carefully before embarking on initiatives that provide financial inputs to communities.

5.4.4 Assist communities in gaining technical and technological support

Protected area agencies and NGOs can play an important role in providing technical and technological support to Community Conserved Areas. These may include support for:

- participatory assessment studies (including mapping and demarcation processes with the use of GIS technologies, for example as described in Box 5.13), visioning, planning, negotiation and evaluation;

- compiling biodiversity inventories and the documentation of ecosystem services and community initiatives (such as the Community Biodiversity Registers maintained by several communities in South Asia); and

- initiatives to support community livelihoods in sustainable ways through the adoption of conservation technologies that are ecologically and socially appropriate and affordable (for instance turtle excluder devices for marine fisherfolk).

---

[142] This is the case for the Associations Villageois de Gestion des Ressources de la Faune (AVIGREF) of Benin, supported by the World Bank: only women are allowed to apply for the post of treasurer (Boukoukenin Tamou Nanti, personal communication, 2002).

> **Checklist 5.5   Examples of economic and financial measures to support Community Conserved Areas**
>
> ▪ Cash and material rewards for outstanding conservation achievements.
>
> ▪ Grants to support specific work for conservation and local livelihoods.
>
> ▪ Financial incentives for conservation, including through compensation for lost opportunities.
>
> ▪ Payment for services rendered by the community to neighbouring communities or the wider world, e.g. protection of water catchment or CO_2 sequestration by forests, maintenance of genetic diversity with actual or potential wider use in agriculture, medicine, industry and other sectors.
>
> ▪ Royalties or fees for the use of genetic resources or related knowledge, developed or maintained by the community.
>
> ▪ Employment in works related to the conservation initiative or other unrelated works.
>
> ▪ Exclusive rights to business initiatives, including tourist accommodation and guiding, trophy hunting, producing and selling handicrafts.

5.4.5   Assist communities in strengthening their institutional structures to manage the Community Conserved Area, or in establishing new ones

Most Community Conserved Areas are governed by one or more institutional structures. They vary in age. Some are traditional bodies, such as indigenous peoples' or village assemblies, which have retained their roles and effectiveness through centuries of existence. Others may be more recently established bodies, such as those set up under formal state-sponsored or donor-sponsored programmes, or community initiatives.

There is also a wide range of institutional structures used to manage Community Conserved Areas. The entire community may be involved in decision-making, or a smaller set of representatives may be assigned this responsibility; those responsible may be mixed gender groups, or groups consisting only of women or men; they may be mostly youth or mostly elders; there may be religious or spiritual groups, or completely secular ones.

It is important to recognise, understand and respect this diversity of institutional arrangements and build upon it, rather than attempting to replace such diversity with uniform, nation-wide institutional structures. This may be a challenge for conservation agencies and any other bodies used to thinking in terms of standard models to be applied across the country or region.

Support to the institutional structures in charge of Community Conserved Areas may involve help to obtain legal recognition (see Section 6), administrative support, financial or material aid to set up an office or take up other functions, training and technical support, support to networking with similar structures (see Section 6.4.3), etc. Any such assistance should ensure that existing arrangements are not undermined. While considerations of social justice, equity and conservation may prompt supporting organizations to attempt to change the nature of the customary or traditional institution, it is a fine line between intervening constructively and interfering in a destructive way. Change can be stimulated from outside, but it should only be carried out with the understanding and support of the concerned community.

Box 5.13 Zoning as a product of a participatory GIS in the Amazon
(adapted from Saragoussi *et al.*, 2002)

Jaú National Park is the largest National Park in Brazil and a World Heritage site. Located in the Amazon region, it is managed through an agreement comprising an environment NGO called Fundação Vitória Amazônica (FVA) and IBAMA, the Brazilian agency responsible for environmental issues. The park residents (locally known as *caboclos* or *riberenos*) have great knowledge about natural resources but are generally illiterate and unaccustomed to deal with modern "management plans" as understood by the authorities in charge. The FVA chose to use a sophisticated Geographical Information System (GIS) as means of involving the community in Jau's management.

Work began by digitising a database. This included physical features of the landscape (vegetation cover, soil types, geology, etc.) taken from secondary data provided by the government. It also included social and economic characteristics of the park resident population, such as natural resource uses, demographic and migration indicators, life history and family relationships – all drawn from primary data collected especially for the database. The information from the residents was collected through participatory assessment exercises and in meetings where concepts such as "planning", "zoning" and "sustainable use" were discussed at length. The information on the use of natural resources was incorporated into maps using small flags depicting vegetal fibres, game animals, fish, turtles etc. These maps were then discussed in workshops among park dwellers, researchers, local decision-makers, and FVA and IBAMA technicians. Finally, the maps were used to delimit the *special use zone*, where extractive activities are now permitted. The remainder of the park was considered a *primitive zone*, except a small area indicated by the dwellers as a *recuperation zone*. Each zone has its own rules of access and use. Currently, the FVA and the local communities are developing further zoning details with clearer day-to-day use decisions. Overall, participatory GIS was shown to a very useful tool, which allowed the integration of information from several sources and the promotion of the engagement of different social actors.

5.4.6 Assist communities in addressing internal and external threats

A Community Conserved Area may face a variety of threats emanating from within or outside the community. Internal challenges can arise from violations of the community rules and ethics by community members. Externally-driven threats include 'development' projects, like mines, dams, roads, industries and urban expansion that threaten the biodiversity protected through the Community Conserved Areas. Other external threats may come from invasive species, pollution, climate change and genetically modified organisms. In some regions, dangers arise from war, ethnic violence and the consequent influxes of refugees and migrants who are not necessarily bound by the local norms and rules.

External threats are hard for the communities to tackle, especially when they come from unknown and/or very powerful sources, and – as globalization processes render commercial-industrial-military forces all the more powerful – communities are under ever greater pressure. Yet, successful struggles against external threats have been waged by communities across the world, at times organized into large mass movements. Sympathetic government agencies, authorities, NGOs and local leaders can play a crucial role in supporting communities facing powerful external threats.

5.4.7 Assist communities in managing conflicts, including conflicts between communities, or between a community and external actors

Most communities have their own mechanisms for resolving or tackling internal conflicts (though some may have been displaced by external mechanisms like courts). However, even when such mechanisms exist, they are often weakly developed or ineffective in the face of external challenges, e.g. conflict between two communities, or between a community and an arm of the state, an industrial enterprise or a mining company. Many Community Conserved Area initiatives have been plagued by conflicts between the conserving community and its less active neighbours. In such situations, external agents like government agencies and NGOs can play a critical role in facilitating the management of such conflict, for example by:

- providing platforms for dialogue on neutral ground;

- making available external, qualified and neutral individuals for arbitration, investigation and communication; or

- facilitating discussion of alternative solutions among the conflicting parties.

Most conflicts between a community and other external actors can be resolved through mediation processes. At times, however, it may be necessary and beneficial to refer to court proceedings and/or to appeal to national or international Truth and Reconciliation Commissions and other human rights mechanisms.

5.4.8 Support local peace processes rooted in indigenous and local agreements on NR management

Violent conflicts bring not only human tragedy – they are also a major obstacle to Community Conserved Areas. They affect local organizational capabilities, disrupt the life of communities, impede participatory governance and often take away the most qualified local leaders. Conflicts also promote internal and external displacements, forcing entire populations to abandon their traditional territories and occupy new territories as refugees, often where they lack a useful knowledge of the environment and local resources. The dynamics of war establish new sets of priorities, with resource conservation and sound ecological management usually at the bottom of the list. This often leads to rapid and unsustainable exploitation of natural resources, usually by newcomers and warring parties, or by peoples with low attachment to the land.

Conflict affects community involvement in conservation in many countries. And yet, community conservation initiatives can be used as an opportunity to identify a common vision of the desired future and create peace-keeping 'laboratories'. Inter-ethnic agreements for conservation and peace-keeping could be used more often for the benefit of both conservation and the relevant communities.[143] The agreements can be promoted and facilitated by external agencies when such agents are seen as neutral with respect to the conflict itself. The external agencies can offer an occasion, a space and a set of basic rules by which the parties can find it easier to come to a mutually satisfactory peace agreement. External agencies are well placed to remind the parties of the importance of sustainable management of the natural resources on which their livelihoods and biodiversity depend.

---

[143] Marco Bassi, personal communication, 2000.

5.5 Help communities to tackle equity issues

The terms "indigenous peoples" and "local communities" sometimes give the impression that these bodies are internally homogenous entities. But in fact they differ greatly along social (access to status), economic (access to resources), and political (access to power) lines. This may result in a range of inequities internal to the communities. Thus women are often disadvantaged compared to men, those without land compared to landowners, the young vis-à-vis the elders, the 'lower' castes relative to the 'higher' ones, and the poorer sections compared to the rich. In mixed communities, indigenous people may be weaker relative to non-indigenous ones. No such inequity is universally valid, but all of them are significant in many countries.

Conservation professionals should be knowledgeable about such inequities, as conservation initiatives may reinforce or reduce them (see Box 5.14). In turn, inequities could have an impact on conservation efforts. For instance, the landless in a village may want to conserve a common property forest as their main source of livelihood, but politically more powerful sections may undermine such initiatives by selling the forest or its timber. Conversely, powerful sectors that may benefit from the ecotourism brought in by conservation may close off poor people's access to the forest, thereby increasing inequities and deprivation. Experience from around the world suggests that it is important to recognise and tackle inequities, both for the long-term sustainability of conservation and to ensure that conservation initiatives do not to lead to further marginalization. And yet, although social justice is a valid objective in itself, national conservation professionals are neither mandated nor equipped to intervene so as to enhance social equity. They should never inflict social engineering on communities, but they should be aware of the intended and unintended consequences of their own work.

5.5.1 Ensure that conservation initiatives reduce, or at least do not reinforce, inequities internal to the community

The dynamic between inequities and conservation policy and practice can be the subject of a joint analysis and dialogue with the people directly affected, who should have the major say in deciding what remedial steps should be taken. As much as possible, efforts to prevent or diminish inequities related to conservation policies and practices should be built on existing community practices. They may involve:

- providing decision-making space to under-privileged groups, e.g. by ensuring their representation on relevant conservation or management bodies;

- helping to improve the capacity of under-privileged groups; and

- ensuring that the benefits of conservation and resource use initiatives accrue in fair proportion to economically or socially under-privileged sections of the community.

Box 5.14   Conservation improves the standing of lower caste people in Saigata Village, India

(adapted from MoEF and Kalpavriksh, in press; Pathak *et al.*, 2004).

The village of Saigata is situated in the central Indian stronghold of *adivasis* (tribal peoples) in the state of Maharashtra. The community is multi-caste, multi-religious and includes tribal and non tribal people such as Adivasi Gonds, Govari, Mana, Mali, Lohar, Dhivar and Kunbis. In the past, the village was surrounded by thick forests, but those forests were all but wiped out between 1955 to 1975 by contractors and villagers themselves. Even villagers started selling fuelwood in the market. Since the 1970s, however, the village has been regenerating and protecting forests under the leadership of an enterprising Dalit (an individual from historically the most disadvantaged section of Indian society). Villagers who grazed their goats and sheep in the forest were convinced to sell their flock voluntarily, and 40 other villagers who earned their livelihood through selling fuelwood started looking for alternative sources of employment.

Since 1993, the village has become part of the official Joint Forest Management Programme of the Maharashtra state. An area of about 270ha is now lush forest with considerable biodiversity, including threatened species like leopards. The fact that the struggle has been led by a person from a "low" caste has increased the standing of disadvantaged people in the village. Elsewhere in India there are other cases where ecological struggle and regeneration have promoted greater social equity. Thus the Chipko (Save the Forests) Movement in the Indian Himalayas has helped women achieve greater respect and decision-making power in general village matters because of their leadership role in forest conservation.

5.5.2   Assist communities in tackling external equity issues, including between the relevant community and neighbouring communities, government agencies and others.

Community conservation initiatives can easily be undermined by a neighbouring community, a government decision or private corporate forces. A single community is often unable to withstand such conflicts, and in such situations external support may be critical to sustain the conservation effort. Government agencies could help the community to stop or regulate the access of outsiders to the community's resources. NGOs could help it to resist a destructive 'development' project that the government or others are proposing for the area. Because of decentralization reforms, local authorities may also be in a strong position to support or impede Community Conserved Areas. For instance, they could formally recognise them or alternatively dis-empower them by imposing "management solutions" upon them.[144] It is essential to analyse the problem with the most directly affected group, and work to identify solutions with them. Measures to reduce or eliminate inequities include:

- giving community representatives a place in relevant decision-making bodies, such as the district, state or national level bodies that are taking decisions on development projects for the area concerned;

- providing powers to the community to restrict or stop outsiders from gaining destructive access to its resources; and

---

[144]   Ferrari and de Vera, 2003.

- making it mandatory for all agencies proposing projects in or around Community Conserved Areas, to hold public hearings, make public all relevant documents, and receive the prior informed consent of affected communities.

6. Overall policy challenges and advice

Legislation and policy regarding natural resource management are crucially important in directing who will manage biodiversity, as well as who will benefit from that management and how. Thus, they provide the foundation for long-term equitable and sustainable relations between government and communities in protected areas. In the absence of appropriate and effective policy, practice can still provide inspiring examples of collaboration and action (and indeed practice is ahead of policy in many cases) but those examples are less than secure.[145]

The current policy milieu regarding recognition and support to community involvement in conservation varies a great deal from region to region and from country to country, and successful policies are generally tailored to the specific context of application. Despite this, it is possible to identify[146] four broad policy recommendations that, across regions, appear to encourage and strengthen the positive contribution of indigenous peoples and local and mobile communities to the conservation of biodiversity, and to protected areas in particular, namely:

1. **strengthen the cultural identity** of indigenous peoples and local and mobile communities, in particular regarding natural resource management and conservation;

2. **secure the rights and responsibilities** of indigenous peoples and local and mobile communities;

3. **ensure legislative and policy backing** to Co-managed Protected Areas and Community Conserved Areas;

4. **support capacity** for co-management and community conservation.

For each of these recommendations some policy options and related advice are discussed below; this is not an exhaustive list.

6.1 Strengthen the cultural identity of indigenous peoples and local and mobile communities, in particular regarding natural resource management and conservation

The natural resource management and conservation systems of indigenous peoples and local and mobile communities, the stability and force of their institutions and the rules

---

[145] It is also true that good policy does not automatically lead to good practice, as implementation capacities and lack of political will often act as obstacles along the way.

[146] This is the result of nine TILCEPA-sponsored regional reviews centred on the role of indigenous and local communities in conservation in different world regions, commissioned and carried out in 2002–2003. The reviews and synthesis paper are available at www.iucn.org/themes/ceesp/Wkg_grp/TILCEPA/community.htm. On this see also Banuri and Najam, 2002.

and practices pertaining to their land and resource use are generally related to the strength of their collective cultural identity. The policy options below are designed to enhance such an identity, in particular regarding natural resource management and conservation.

Policy options

6.1.1 Document and re-affirm the cultural dimension of conservation

Conservation policies can support the documentation, valuing and practical use of various aspects of community involvement in conservation and local links between cultural and biological diversity. This involves gathering and disseminating information, for example through videos and audiocassettes that record interviews with community elders. It also involves research on indigenous knowledge, land-use systems and institutional arrangements that are often as sophisticated as they are poorly understood and documented.[147] It involves paying more attention to the cultural roots of conservation in training institutions and manuals for natural resource managers. Policies can also promote awareness of the cultural dimension of conservation using dedicated conferences, publications, media attention, etc.

6.1.2 Respect and employ existing ethnic and local natural resource management systems

Ethnic and local systems of natural resource management involve complex combinations of: norms (e.g. customary law); procedures (e.g. decisional processes, conflict management and dispute settlement); knowledge, resources, skills and institutions (e.g. councils of elders); and individuals playing specific roles (often the traditional leaders). Most such systems represent tailored responses to the particular interactions between local ecosystems, habitats and species and local communities. Policies to revitalize and strengthen such systems require a combination of moral respect and material support. This begins with appropriate efforts at documentation (see option 6.1.1) and requires a basic personal respect (language, etiquette) in interaction with traditional leaders. It also requires that authority and responsibility for specific functions and tasks be shared between community institutions and state bodies. Policies, for instance, could value and employ community capacities though a preferential use of indigenous and community experts and could support the application of local knowledge, skills and technologies in natural resource management. Importantly, policies should discourage agencies and projects from imposing pre-conceived organizational models on communities[148] and rather allow indigenous peoples and local and mobile communities to organize according to the models that best suit their culture and needs. The *ecological* as well as the social dangers of a top down approach are illustrated in Box 6.1.

---

[147] ... and at times even thought as "primitive" or "destructive".

[148] It is common for conservation projects to impose on communities the creation of "local committees" to manage natural resources whose composition is determined by the project designers. Such committees often perform poorly and may engender social disruptions and conflicts. In several countries, the structure of contemporary indigenous organizations was imposed at colonial times (examples are the *Cabildos* in Ecuador and the *Capitanias* in Bolivia).

6.1.3 Promote broad social respect for indigenous peoples and local and mobile communities, starting from new and culture-sensitive school curricula

This policy option goes well beyond the subject of conservation as it deals with generating wider respect for indigenous peoples and local and mobile communities within the society-at-large. This, however, provides a crucially important context if communities are to be encouraged to value their own capacities for conservation and other livelihood objectives. The re-orientation of school curricula could help to promote an appreciation of cultural pluralism, and of the unique values and capacities of each culture. A pluralist perspective on history and a thoughtful, non-ideological analysis of the pros and cons of development processes should underpin the development process in general.

More specifically in the area of conservation, protected area agencies, NGOs etc. can help by working with schools programmes to include field visits to communities engaged in managing their natural resources; and by supporting "community-based environmental education initiatives" that at times make use of Community Conserved Areas as environmental education centres.[149]

Box 6.1   Top down rule or local knowledge?
(from Biksham Gujja, personal communication, 2003)

In Rajastan (India), Keoladeo National Park is a natural depression re-designed by local kings (e.g., via small dams) to attract as many birds as possible. Throughout centuries of careful water management, the site became an internationally famous bird sanctuary and began attracting more and more visitors. These wetlands are also World Heritage and Ramsar sites. In 1982, after declaring the site as National Park, the government constructed a three metres wall topped with barbed wire around it to prevent access to people and, most importantly, to stop buffalo grazing. Grazing, in fact, is not legally allowed inside Indian National Parks. These measures were implemented without consultation with the local communities, who saw their historical pattern of access and use suddenly becoming illegal. Years of violent conflict, non-cooperation and passive resistance ensued. Several people died in numerous protest actions.

Several years later, however, an expensive scientific study "discovered" that buffalo grazing is essential for the maintenance of the ecological characteristics that actually attract the birds, something that the local peoples had known and fought for all along! With the help of WWF, a new atmosphere of dialogue and collaboration is finally developing between the park management and the local communities. A number of agreements have been drawn to regulate fodder collection and access to temples inside the park. Some welfare measures have been initiated by park authorities and the tourist fees to visit the Park have been increased. The Park authorities are reported to be willing to allow controlled grazing inside the park, sharing of tourist revenues with the local communities and setting up effective joint management schemes. However, the situation is still not entirely clear as national park policy in India does not permit these kinds of agreements. So, while on the ground several such initiatives to engage local communities have resulted in agreements that are beneficial to people and ecosystem alike, there is a need to modify the national legal framework governing protected areas so as to provide an institutionally secure foundation for such agreements.

---

[149]   An example is the Malaysian village of Kampong Endah. The village has its own Environmental Awareness Activity Centre run by the villagers themselves, which has been carrying out medicinal plants programmes, clean up campaigns, recycling competitions, nature camps for schools and the public, and other activities with the active participation of all social groups in the village. Successful sessions based on traditional practices are carried out to revitalize and appreciate local culture. Visitors come from all over Malaysia and abroad (Ferrari, 2002).

Other ways to overcome dominant-society lack of information and opposition to traditional values and lifestyles include promoting dialogues between community representatives and sensitive experts trained in modern technologies (radio and TV programmes can be very useful here) as well as documentaries, reports, and well-produced fiction (e.g. street theatre, soap operas) showing with understanding and respect the cultural differences that enrich society. At the most basic level, this policy option ought to be grounded in the country's constitution, which should assign to all citizens the same basic rights and social respect. In addition, however, some form of "affirmative action" may be necessary, for example to counteract the effects of racist beliefs and of forms of primary education that ignore, or denigrate, traditional cultural values. Though such measures go far beyond conservation and are desirable for many other reasons, they will help to create the environment which is conducive to community-based conservation.

6.1.4 Promote the survival and vitality of local languages

Traditional knowledge, customary laws and institutions, and biodiversity names and uses are interconnected and inseparable from local languages and dialects. In this sense, the survival and vitality of indigenous and local languages acquire a central role in maintaining alive entire bodies of cultural and biological knowledge.[150] Efforts at saving languages that are on the way to extinction are thus extremely important to conservation.[151] Protected area agencies can help here by adopting policies on the use of local languages at meetings, in official documents, in educational programmes, etc. A simple measure of great value for conservation is to maintain, respect and restore the local, ethnic names of species and places, and of protected areas in particular.[152]

6.2 Secure the rights of indigenous peoples and local and mobile communities

Indigenous and local and mobile communities are the "natural" and most ancient managers of natural resources. It is around such resources (a forest, a watershed, a rich coastal stretch, a wetland, a landscape suited for grazing …) that they developed as social units and evolved distinct cultural traits in response to common opportunities and challenges. These ancient relationships are the roots of the perceived rights of indigenous peoples and of local and mobile communities to land and natural resources. Yet, many contemporary communities seem to have "lost" such rights. The process started centuries ago, with the so-called "enclosure of the commons"[153] by which

---

[150] An organization dedicated to exploring and acting upon this relationship is www.terralingua.org.

[151] The People's Organization of Tinangol, Sabah (Malaysia), for example, started a programme to introduce the local Rungus language into their kindergarten and have just finished preparing the first kindergarten book in Rungus. To complement this, an elderly volunteer teaches the Rungus language once a week to village adults who are interested in rediscovering their mother tongue (Ferrari, 2002).

[152] Very often, protected area managers and agencies replace traditional names of places with foreign names that have no meaning for the people of the region. In the Southern Andes of Ecuador, for example, local people use the name *romerillo* to refer to a specific species of tree. Yet when a National Park was established in an area with many *romerillo* trees, protected area planners decided to name the area after the Latin name for the species (*Podocarpus* spp.), instead of the local name, resulting in "Podocarpus National Park" – a name that means nothing to local people.

[153] See, for instance, Polanyi, 1957.

powerful and wealthy individuals seized common lands and brought them into what they considered to be more productive and profitable uses. Later on, nation states, often through specialized agencies, seized more "national lands and resources" for development and conservation purposes. Finally, individual and corporate owners and even well-meaning conservation NGOs have bought land and resources, with a special eye for those places that have great biodiversity and tourism value.

Much of this change – which is global, and of truly historical proportions – happened without regard to the customary rights of indigenous peoples and local and mobile communities. In some places, mostly in the developed world, the process is basically completed and community ownership and resource management have been almost entirely replaced by those of the state and individual and corporate land-owners, who have thus become the managers of natural resources. In other countries, mostly those in the South, the process remains unfinished and contested, and a conflict-rich interface exists between traditional (community-based) and "modern" (state and property-based) natural resource management systems. Issues related to the rights of communities go beyond the concern of the conservation sector, but some controversies are particularly relevant to conservation, such as those concerning land and resources incorporated within official protected areas through the forced eviction of their original residents. Today, several governments are approaching the problem of restitution of the relevant rights, although it is often impossible to "go back" to the original conditions and restitution processes need to be coupled with other initiatives. This is a unique occasion for agencies and communities to develop strong and effective conservation alliances.

Policy options

6.2.1 Recognise the right of indigenous peoples and local and mobile communities to self-determination and prior informed consent on conservation initiatives affecting traditional territories and, in particular, their Community Conserved Areas

Countries that have undertaken to implement the CBD and ratified the ILO Convention 169 are increasingly facing consideration of the rights of self-determination and prior informed consent on matters of natural resource management. Policies that recognise communities as legal entities and transfer to them authority and responsibility for land and resource management contribute to the right to self-determination. Examples include statutory legislation that recognises the collective rights of indigenous peoples, various forms of local autonomy, devolution measures (see Box 6.2), support for communities to demarcate and protect their land and resources against various forms of threats and the provision of legal advice to speed up procedures for legal titling of community lands.[154] In conflict situations over natural resources, some formal recogni-tion of 'primary' rights to land (property or permanent usufruct) could be provided to communities with a long-standing local interest and who practice an ecologically sound model of sustainable resource use. This could help them re-affirm their rights versus

---

[154] The establishment of the Amarakaeri communal reserve in Peru was delayed because of practical problems in getting government officials to clarify land tenure issues in the area. This could have been sped up with more consistent and effective legal support (FENAMAD, 2002).

newcomers and opportunistic users.[155] At the international level, relevant policies may involve supporting the work of the UN Working Group on Indigenous Peoples and its Permanent Forum on Indigenous Issues.[156]

6.2.2 Recognise land and resource rights and security of tenure in all cases where indigenous and community lands overlap with protected areas, including via land restitution processes, as necessary

Policies that recognise customary rights with respect to protected areas begin with the statutory requirement for agreements between state governments and concerned communities *prior* to protected area establishment. Also very important is the recognition of communities as legitimate co-managers in government-established protected areas and as full managers in Community Conserved Areas (see 6.3 below). In line with CBD decisions,[157] conservation policies can explicitly renounce forcible resettlement of indigenous peoples (possibly extended to traditional local communities) and forcible 'sedentarisation' (or settlement) of mobile indigenous peoples for the purpose of establishing protected areas. In place of this, policies can support communities to make informed decisions through participatory processes for assessing, planning and evaluating development and conservation initiatives.

Where protected areas already exist, the thorniest issues often concern vulnerable natural resources that are essential for the physical or cultural survival of the communities holding traditional rights. These resources may be located far from the state-recognised "residence" of the relevant communities: this is especially so in the case of mobile indigenous peoples. The challenge, for policy and practice, is to develop tailored agreements among community, private and state interests that manage to re-affirm both the rights of conservation and the rights of communities. Examples of such

---

Box 6.2   Decentralization, delegation and devolution
(adapted from Ribot, 2002)

Decentralization is an act by which a central government formally cedes power to actors and institutions at lower levels in a political-administrative and territorial hierarchy. If the actors and institutions are local branches of the central state (e.g. prefectures, local administration and technical ministries) the process is often referred to as "administrative decentralization" or "de-concentration". If they are private bodies such as individuals, corporations or NGOs, the process is called "privatization" or *"delegation"*. If they are local authorities downwardly accountable to local people, the process is called "democratic decentralization" or *"devolution"*.[158]

The powers that can be transferred are: legislative (elaboration of rules), executive (implementing and enforcing decisions), financial and judicial. These powers and the financial resources to implement actions are rarely transferred together in integrated packages that could create positive synergies, a fact that complicates the process and can generate conflicts.

---

[155]   Bassi, 2003.

[156]   MacDonald, 2003.

[157]   CBD Programme of Work on Protected Areas, COP 7, Kuala Lumpur, 2004.

[158]   Adapted from Ribot, 2002; and Alcorn *et al.*, 2003.

agreements are being developed around the globe[159] on the basis of land restitution and devolution of wildlife management rights – see for example Box 6.3. Such policies do not mean that land and wildlife are lost to conservation. On the contrary, communities often choose to retain their land under a protected area status and/or set up sustainable use rules (an example is described in Box 6.4). Governments willing to go this route may wish to set up a legal advisory service, specialized in land rights, to assist communities to secure their reparation.

6.2.3 Clarify and protect the Intellectual Property Rights of indigenous peoples and local and mobile communities regarding biological resources in protected areas and Community Conserved Areas

Control over the collection and use of information is a major concern for people whose livelihoods depend on traditional knowledge and skills.[160] Countries that are signatories to the CBD have an obligation to develop policies that safeguard the traditional knowledge and practices of indigenous and local communities, and ensure that such practices and

---

Box 6.3 Co-management with Even reindeer herders, Kytalyk Resource Reserve, Russia
(adapted from Larsen, 2000 and Beltrán, 2000)

A co-management agreement has been negotiated between Even community delegates and the Yakutian Ministry for Natural Protection in eastern Siberia, Russia. This involves the establishment of a Trustee Co-ordinating Council, which includes Even representatives but also employs Even reindeer herders in the ranger service. Under the agreement, a number of rules have been drawn up:

- The indigenous population uses this area mostly in the winter, and leaves all the gear in the hunter's cabins (traps and nets). The administration of Kytalyk Reserve undertakes to protect the fishing and trapping grounds and all the gear in the summertime, when the main nesting habitats of the Siberian White Crane are closed to the public (a zone of 624,625ha will be left entirely undisturbed through the season).

- Areas with no significant concentration of nesting white cranes acquire the status of a Traditional Nature Resource Use Zone (141,050ha). In these areas, hunting of aquatic birds and waterfowl is banned, as is unauthorized access for people not related to traditional land use.

- At the request of the indigenous people, the world-renowned mammoth cemetery at Berelyakh has been included in the reserve territory (6,570ha of sacred lands). The indigenous population has always worshipped this area, but lately the mammoth burial ground has been subject to vandalism by tourists and businessmen.

- The reserve will have an area for licensed wild reindeer hunting (28,125ha). This is a traditional hunting area for one of the family communities. The reserve will also have a small area where licensed fishing is allowed (7,000ha).

- Tracts of the eastern Siberian seacoast, including the Indigirka River Delta (800,000ha), are to receive the status of a Reserved Territory.[161]

---

[159] An example related to the Huichol indigenous communities in the state of San Luis Potosi (Mexico) is described in Box 5.10. Legal frameworks at the regional level may need to be adapted to understand, accept and protect traditional access use rights, and to facilitate the implementation of measures to enforce them.

[160] Dermot Smyth, personal communication, 2003.

[161] For a fuller account, see Beltrán, 2000.

Box 6.4   Balancing the powers in Makuleke land
(adapted from Steenkamp, 2002)

In 1969, the Makuleke community of the Limpopo Province was forcibly removed from a tract of land in the north-eastern corner of South Africa. Their land was incorporated into the Kruger National Park and the community relocated some 70km towards the south. Close to thirty years later, ownership of the land was returned to them by way of a co-management agreement with the South African National Parks (SANP). This settlement was negotiated under the auspices of the land reform programme launched by South Africa's first post-apartheid government.

Land ownership gave the Makuleke substantial bargaining weight and the settlement fundamentally changed the balance of power between the two parties. The agreement made it possible for the Makuleke to pursue their interests in the land relative to those of the SANP and the state. It also created a secure framework for the longer-term conservation of the exceptional biodiversity of the Makuleke land. The implementation of the agreement did not take place without intervening conflicts, but all tensions were ultimately dealt with within the framework of the agreement.

---

knowledge are used by the wider society only with the consent of the relevant communities and through equitable benefit-sharing arrangements. Even in the absence of specific legislation that recognises and protects intellectual property rights, there exist ways of safeguarding these rights through specific agreements and procedures.[162] These are of particular relevance as part of protected area co-management arrangements.

6.2.4   Promote sound governance in conservation at all levels, from the local community to the national government

Sound governance is a complex concept involving respect for human rights, issues of fair participation, transparency and accountability in decision-making, equity in the sharing of costs and benefits of decisions, performance and vision.[163] The principle of "subsidiarity" – which calls on governments to decentralize/delegate/devolve[164] authority and responsibilities to the lowest possible level with capacity to assume responsibility for the relevant social tasks – is also considered an indicator of sound governance.[165]

The CBD has called attention to issues of governance in its COP 7 Programme of Work on Protected Areas. Protected area policy can foster improvements in conservation governance at various levels, from local communities to national policy-making bodies. To begin with, it could promote the participatory evaluation of governance structures, practices and mechanisms as they relate to individual protected area and protected area systems.[166] The evaluation exercises would identify strengths to celebrate

---

[162]   Laird, 2002.

[163]   Graham *et al.*, 2003.

[164]   See Box 6.1 for a definition of these terms.

[165]   The subsidiarity principle has been re-affirmed by several national and international documents and agreements, including the guidelines for community involvement in protected area management developed by WCPA, IUCN and WWF (Beltrán, 2000) and some IUCN Resolutions. Enhancing local autonomy in defining landscapes, managing natural resources and planning and implementing development and conservation initiatives is a powerful means to awaken and utilise the capacities of civil society.

[166]   Abrams *et al.*, 2003.

and problems to address. Typical governance problems encountered in relation to protected areas are scarce stakeholder participation, poor transparency and accountability in decision-making and unfair sharing of the costs and benefits of conservation. These can be addressed by policies that establish participatory management regimes (such as Co-managed Protected Areas, see Box 6.3) and foster the more equitable sharing of conservation benefits (see Box 6.5). Interestingly, some communities in areas beset by governance problems have started to establish Community Conserved Areas in an effort to protect at least a portion of their territories and resources from mismanagement and corruption.[167]

Box 6.5   Who enjoys the benefits of conservation? Who bears the costs?

From the perspective of *some* communities, the establishment of protected areas has made enormous positive changes in terms of their own identity, security and economic capacity. Some protected areas have enshrined in national legislation the rights of indigenous peoples to live in and manage certain territories.[168] Others have helped poor communities economically, for instance by providing the basis for flourishing tourism-based industries.[169] And still others have protected the natural resources that the local communities depend on, and which would otherwise be at risk from destructive external forces.

   In other cases, however, indigenous peoples and local and mobile communities harbour a sense of resentment, distrust and resistance towards the protected areas in their midst. Obvious examples include communities that were forced to relocate or curtail traditional resource uses because of the establishment of the protected areas, with the consequent disruption of their livelihoods and well-being. This is why some commentators maintain that the cumulative negative impact of protected areas may have been underestimated.[170]

   With more or less strength, depending on their own organising abilities, many affected indigenous and local communities have been claiming for the recognition of past inequities and the redress of injustices. In a few cases, this has led to land restitution from protected areas which were established without their prior informed consent – restitution is in fact slowly becoming more common.[171] Constitutional recognition of such rights would get them involved as "rightful partners" in protected area management but it may take longer for them to secure tangible benefits, even after the establishment of participatory management structures.[172] In other cases, the local protected area administrators have responded by agreeing to distribute some "conservation benefits" to local communities, though this has not always been done with their involvement.[173] Action of this kind includes adding a develop-ment component to conservation initiatives,[174] allowing the communities to extract carefully determined quantities of resources, for instance in the buffer zones,[175] or sharing with communities a fixed percentage of tourism revenues from the protected area.[176] It can only be judged on a case-by-case basis whether these measures are equitable and effective.

---

[167]   This, for instance, has been happening in Cambodia (Ferrari, 2002).

[168]   Zuluaga *et al.*, 2003.

[169]   The Parco Nazionale d'Abruzzo, in Italy, managed to rescue an entire region from secular economic under-development.

[170]   Cernea and Schmidt-Soltau, 2003.

[171]   See Box 6.2.

[172]   Larsen, 2000.

[173]   Borrini-Feyerabend and Sandwith, 2003.

[174]   Worah, 2002.

[175]   Okello *et al.*, 2003,

[176]   Bajimaja, 2003; Luckett *et al.*, 2003.

6.3 Ensure crucial legislative and policy backing to Co-managed Protected Areas and Community Conserved Areas

Poor collaboration between communities and conservation agencies is often rooted in the lack of supportive laws and policies, despite the existence of broad and vague intentions to "enhance community participation". Sometimes protected area staff are placed in a difficult position, being encouraged to experiment in participation, but offered little in terms of new resources and left to bear the responsibility of the consequences. Yet collaboration between conservation agencies and communities is crucial. It can be fostered through a range of policies that can be tailored to the specific situation.

Policy options

6.3.1 Promote the formal recognition of indigenous peoples and local and mobile communities, and of the diversity of their customary collective institutions

National legislation and policies may or may not be oriented to involve communities in conservation. This is because civil law varies in several crucial aspects. First, it may or may not recognise the existence and peculiar characteristics and rights of *indigenous peoples* in the country. Second, it may or may not offer a legal status to *natural communities* (and not only to formal associations of individuals, such as cooperatives). Third, it may or may not recognise the *collective rights and responsibilities* of such communities (including security of tenure over natural resources). Recognition of indigenous peoples, natural communities and collective rights and responsibilities are basic legal and policy conditions to secure community engagement in conservation. When these are still wanted, specific proposals and amendments need to be developed and information on them disseminated, especially among lawmakers and politicians (see Box 6.6), to raise awareness of the relevant opportunities and obstacles to community engagement in conservation.[177] And even where there is favourable legislation, it may need to be better disseminated and implemented.[178]

In shaping laws and policies, the complexity of customary natural resource management systems should not be underestimated. Policies to support them should be flexible enough to allow site-specific arrangements through which communities can retain or develop their own institutional and management arrangements rather than being forced to follow a single national model. Developing appropriate laws and policies will often require in-depth participatory analyses of existing natural resource management systems, along with dialogue and agreements among all parties concerned.[179] For conservation purposes, it is useful to recall that a lack of recognition of local customary institutions has often undermined the sense of territorial security required to substantiate community commitments to conservation and aggravated or prompted conflicts. In recognition of this, several countries have adopted legal provisions and measures to devolve conflict management responsibilities to traditional institutions on matters related to land/water and

---

[177] This is particularly important in countries deriving their legal tradition from Roman Law, where incorporation of customary ruling tends to be more difficult than in common-law countries.

[178] In India, for instance, the government has repeatedly not publicized and sometimes not implemented the devolutionary laws and policies approved by the Parliament (Pathak, 2003).

Box 6.6 Recognising indigenous and local communities as legal entities – a crucial step towards engaging them in conservation

Policies are not always the principal reason why the relationship between communities and conservation is problematic. At times, deeper and more structural obstacles are found in legislation (e.g. civil code, rural code, pastoral code) that does not officially recognise indigenous and local communities as legal entities and cannot therefore accommodate their collective rights and responsibilities. According to some legislation, only individuals, businesses and the state "exist". Rarely is there a simple and effective legal status for natural communities willing to manage and conserve their natural resources. Even rarer is a legal status that allows local communities not only to manage resources, but to derive an economic profit from them "as a community".

Local collective rights and responsibilities are at the core of land tenure and resource access patterns in most traditional societies. They are usually designed to accommodate multiple and changing needs and are based on a mosaic of land uses that include conservation but are not limited to it. From a conservation perspective, collective – as opposed to individual rights and responsibilities – can be very beneficial. In physical terms, they tend to avoid fragmentation, maintaining the land's ecological integrity and conserving biodiversity. In social terms, they provide a strong basis for the maintenance and functioning of community institutions, indispensable for long-term management. They also strengthen the role of customary law as related to land management and of traditional knowledge as applied to broader territorial and landscape units. Most traditional collective tenure systems have been altered by successive interventions that appropriated ("enclosed") land into private property or state-property and erased collective forms of tenure. Moreover, in much of the world, collective customary rights have weak legal recognition.[180] In some cases even the community memory of collective rights and responsibilities has eroded, due to cultural change and the dominating influence of individual rights and formal law. In some countries, however, these collective tenure systems continue to this day, usually in the form of traditional rights and responsibilities extending over specific territories and resources and recognised as essential components of local culture and livelihoods.[181] In others they are being revived as part of decentralization and devolution policies.[182]

---

[179] For instance, customary/ethnic governance systems often ascribe land and resource tenure to several actors at the same time. These include families, extended families, villages, lineages, clans, etc. Thus attempting to prescribe a single level of property or use rights for empowerment and planning purposes is to over-simplify a complex issue. Usually, customary land use patterns recognise overlapping claims on a given territory, and such claims are connected to collective identities of different importance and defined by different types of rights. Most often, the overall regulating unit has an ethnic basis – the sharing of a common identity and cultural values – and elaborates specific devices (norms on circulation of people and access to resources, decisional councils, rituals, myths, etc.) to ensure sustainable livelihoods. An ethnic group is thus in control and solves conflicts within its own structure of authority.

[180] Do customary tenure systems have to be formally codified? From the perspective of traditional cultures and communities it would appear that the answer is 'no', as such systems are generally well understood and accepted in the specific local context. From the perspective of the broader society, however, codification may be needed so that all actors, within and outside the communities, know, accept, value and respect them. If the answer is 'yes', then, which collective rights and responsibilities would be best codified? Some communities wish to revitalize collective land tenure over historical monuments or symbolic natural features to strengthen their own sense of identity and social values. Others wish to retain collective tenure over "extensive" resources, such as high-altitude grazing areas, forests, water or fisheries but prefer individual ownership over "intensive use" resources, such as agricultural land. Importantly, formally recognised collective rights and responsibilities may be essential for Community Conserved Areas and Co-managed Protected Areas (see also Oviedo, 2002).

[181] Roldan, 2002; Plant and Hvalkof, 2001.

[182] Maldidier, 2000.

resource use, particularly where these concern internal conflicts and relationships with neighbouring communities.[183]

6.3.2 Ensure legitimacy and support to communities willing to engage in Co-managed Protected Areas

Several types of legislation and policy can provide support to communities to participate effectively in protected area co-management arrangements.

The first type of supportive legislation is at a very broad, constitutional level. In this sense, civil law may recognise the right of citizens to participate in decision-making processes and governance bodies at various levels.[184] In addition to voting and delegated democracy, the principle of subsidiarity[185] can be explicitly enshrined in law and pursued through decentralization, delegation and devolution policies (see Box 6.2). Basic law can also ensure free access to information, including information related to the management of natural resources and to the protection of the environment. An example from Europe, with potentially wider application, is given in Box 6.7. As mentioned in 6.3.1, the basic provisions need also to recognise indigenous peoples and local and mobile communities as legal subjects with customary rights and characteristic relationship to national resources. A national legal and policy framework comprising such provisions most naturally supports co-management processes for natural resources in general and for protected areas in particular.

The second type is legislation and policy that does not specifically address protected areas but has an impact on them. This includes national level financial and economic policy (including trade policy) that can be geared towards equity rather than profit and designed to combat poverty, putting limits to the concentration of economic power in production and supply sectors and reducing social and economic inequality. As part of this, economic incentives (e.g. tax rebates, jobs, economic opportunities, easements, priority considerations in development planning) can be given to communities willing to engage in conservation. And market mechanisms can be devised to combine ecological certification, socio-cultural certification, and fair trade networks.[186]

The third type is national legislation specifically for protected areas. Such legislation can, for instance, require that all protected areas in the country be governed by a Management Board composed of representatives of the key relevant actors (as in the case of a number of countries referred to in Chapter 4). Or the national system for the classification of protected areas could reflect various degrees and forms of community

---

[183] In many countries, the water management authority has been appropriated by state governments from communities and local landowners, with the argument that water is a resource of national interest. In spite of good intentions, the demise of traditional rights and responsibilities that used to regulate water use and sharing, especially in mountain and other areas subject to cyclical scarcity, can create a sense of insecurity and may rekindle or prompt conflicts among communities. Following this, some countries, notably in South America, devolved conflict-management responsibilities to traditional institutions on matters related to land and water resource use (Oviedo, 2002). This could be implemented with success in other countries.

[184] Borrini-Feyerabend *et al.*, 2004 (in press).

[185] See section 6.2.4 above.

[186] The Awa people of Ecuador, for instance, have developed a powerful benefit-generation system through sustainable forest management. A community institution controls trading of timber and non-timber products, handles certification processes, and maintains links with fair trade markets.

Box 6.7   The Aarhus (UN/ECE) Convention on Access to Information, Public Participation in Decision-Making and Access to Justice in Environmental Matters

(adapted from WRI, 2003)

The Aarhus Convention is an environmental treaty that turns the 1992 Rio Declaration's vague commitments to the principles of access to information into specific legal obligations. Since its negotiation in 1998 (at Aarhus, Denmark) as a regional agreement among the countries of the United Nations Economic Commission for Europe (UNECE), 24 nations in Europe and Central Asia have become Parties to the treaty, and 40 have signed it. The treaty entered into force in October 2001, and is now open to signature by all nations of the world.

The Aarhus Convention recognises the basic right of every person of present and future generations to a healthy environment and specifies how the authorities at all levels will provide fair and transparent decision-making processes, access to information, and access to redress. For example, the convention requires broad access to information about the state of air and atmosphere, water, land, and biological diversity; information about influences on the environment such as energy, noise, development plans, and policies; and information about how these influences affect human health and safety. A person does not need to prove "legal standing" to request information or to comment on official decisions that affect the environment, and the convention requires that governments respond to requests for information from any person of any nationality *within one month*. The convention also gives citizens, organizations, and governments the right to investigate and seek to curtail pollution caused by public and private entities in other countries that are parties to the treaty. For example, a Hungarian public interest group could demand information on airborne emissions from a Czech factory. For most signatory countries, meeting the standards of the treaty will require authorities to change how they disseminate environmental information to the public, to create new systems of environmental reporting by businesses and government, to improve the practice of public notification and comment, and to change judicial processes.

Adopting and implementing the Aarhus Convention's principles beyond its European base could provide a straightforward route to better access to information at a global level. But while there is growing interest in endorsing the Aarhus principles in Latin America, southern Africa, and the Asia-Pacific region, many countries perceive the treaty's concepts of democratic decision-making about the environment as too liberal or threatening to commercial confidentiality. Some countries are also reluctant to adopt a treaty that they did not have a chance to shape initially. Nonetheless, the Aarhus Convention stands as an example of real progress toward a global understanding of what access is and how it can be manifested in national laws and practices.

involvement in the management of natural resources.[187] Even in the absence of legislation to this effect, policies could be "experimented with" in pilot sites.

Finally, a policy framework of great importance for co-management is at the level of international instruments and agreements, such as international conventions or provisions, guidelines and conditionality established in bilateral relationships. In many respects, the most fundamental international instrument in support of co-management

---

[187]   By an amendment to its Wild Life (Protection) Act in 2002, India expanded its protected area system to include two new categories in addition to national parks and sanctuaries: community reserves and conservation reserves. Both were intended to expand the role of communities in conservation. However, the provisions related to these new categories are extremely restrictive and would not go far in achieving this objective (Pathak and Bhushan, 2004).

remains the Universal Declaration of Human Rights (UDHR), but in recent years international agreements have specifically addressed issues of governance, participation, equity and benefit sharing in the management of natural resources and protected areas in particular. The most important of these is the CBD Programme of Work on Protected Areas (see Chapter 2), adopted in 2004. All these instruments stress the need to reconcile protection and sustainable use and provide the conditions for communities to engage fully in natural resource management and conservation.

6.3.3 Ensure legitimacy and support to communities willing to manage Community Conserved Areas and recognise their contributions to national protected area systems, transboundary protected areas and international conservation agreements

National policies can strengthen community conservation initiatives through various forms of formal recognition. This could begin by some national inventory[188] followed by local consultation and decision making at the level of each Community Conserved Area, which should allow the expression of a variety of concerns and entitlements. Great care should be taken so that the original community purposes and means are not distorted or under-valued in the process.[189] The most straightforward arrangements are possible when communities are recognised as legal entities and can be entrusted with the authority and responsibility to conserve their common land and resources in continuity with established patterns and structures. Where this is not legally feasible, some innovative ways of recognising Community Conserved Areas have been devised.[190] An especially important step is for appropriate Community Conserved Areas to be "incorporated" in the national system of protected areas (as is clearly encouraged now in the CBD Protected Areas Programme of Work),[191] as well as receiving support though recognition of their role in National Biodiversity Strategy and Action Plans.[192] Policies that achieve this allow an important level of protection to Community Conserved Areas (for instance, they can help to fend off the negative impact of large scale development initiatives on local livelihoods and conservation systems).[193]

---

[188] This is being done, or at least initiated by NGOs, in Australia, Colombia, India, Iran and Italy.

[189] Community Conserved Areas should remain under the management and control of the relevant communities and be allowed to retain their primary management purpose (which may not be conservation *per se* but actually achieve conservation). Established local institutions and practices should be respected and not tampered with, though they might be "renamed" as necessary to garner legal recognition. In some cases, territories and resources are regularly visited/"used" and "managed" by several communities. This is the case for sacred mountains or rivers, at times distant from the communities' permanent settlements but nevertheless places of fundamental importance to them. Communities are extremely reluctant to accept a loss of rights over these areas, even when they recognise that they cannot have full ownership over them. Creative solutions need to be found in these cases, for example in the form of joint use agreements and declarations of a 'Joint Community Conserved Area'.

[190] In Kenya, the elders guardians of the Kaya forests have retained a primary role in protecting their forests through national legislation on Natural Monuments backed by the legal and field assistance provided by an external project. In other cases, communities acquired a legal status by establishing themselves as an association or private corporation to manage their own conserved areas. This helps overcome bureaucratic obstacles but also runs the risk of distorting the nature of the management system. Interim strategies can also be developed to allow Community Conserved Areas to acquire some form of recognition in the short and medium term, thereby allowing for *de facto* solutions to be put in place while *de jure* solutions are in the making.

[191] Borrini-Feyerabend, 2003; Oviedo, 2003a.

[192] The final technical report of the National Biodiversity Strategy and Action Plan in India, for instance, devotes an entire section to Community Conserved Areas, recommending a series of actions for documenting, studying, supporting, and giving legal backing to such initiatives (MoEF and Kalpavriksh, 2004, in press).

At the international level, the following steps could help to raise the profile of Community Conserved Areas:

- Where appropriate, recognising them as transboundary protected areas (this is particularly important for the traditional migration territories of mobile indigenous peoples), or as part of such transboundary areas.[194]

- Draw on appropriate decisions of multilateral environmental agreements and instruments, such as the CBD, Wetlands of International Importance (Ramsar), World Heritage, and the Man and Biosphere Programme of UNESCO, to legitimize and support community conservation.

- Act on the recommendation adopted at the Durban World Parks Congress (5.19) that called for a revision of the 1994 Guidelines on Protected Area Management Categories to include a way of showing how protected areas, "which are assigned to their category by primary management objectives, can also be described by reference to the organization responsible for their governance ... "

- Provide data on those Community Conserved Areas that are recognised as protected areas to the World Database of Protected Areas (held by UNEP-World Conservation Monitoring Centre), while ensuring that any sensitive information is included only with the prior informed consent of the community concerned.

6.3.4 Involve communities in conservation policy and planning and promote the integration of Community Conserved Areas within their landscapes/ seascapes

Policies can support the involvement of communities[195] in policy and planning exercises for sustainable development and conservation at various administrative levels and geographical scales, specifically in national and sub-national fora dedicated to natural resource management and biodiversity conservation (e.g. in National Biodiversity Strategy and Action Plans). Through direct representation, communities can argue for their Community Conserved Areas to be recognised and included in landscape/seascape conservation policies and plans, legitimizing their experience and promoting better conservation practices overall.

---

[193] The IUCN Recommendation 2.82 from the Amman World Conservation Congress (2000) calls for a total prohibition on mining inside protected areas of Categories I to IV, and naturally applies to those Community Conserved Areas that are recognised as protected area in those categories.

[194] The contribution that can be made by transboundary initiatives to support the efforts of local communities to conserve biodiversity is described in Sandwith *et al.*, 2001.

[195] In India, for instance, several village forest councils (*van panchayats)* in the state of Uttaranchal, and dozens of forest protection committees in the state of Orissa, have come together to press for common demands, exchange experiences, and strengthen each others' initiatives. It is important in such cases that community representatives be allowed to participate in their own language and with their own parameters of discourse, to ensure that they are not simply token participants at meetings and in decision-making processes. It is also important that Community Conserved Area representatives be chosen by the communities themselves rather than by outside agencies.

6.4 Support agency and community capacities for co-management and community conservation

"Capacities" comprise complex combinations of attitudes, knowledge, skills, resources and institutions, and depend on a supportive context for their application. Governments and other social actors willing to support the conservation role of indigenous peoples and local and mobile communities are therefore challenged first to recognise and understand these capacities, and then to provide the enabling legal and political context for their application. Through policies, they can also encourage and support the *improvement* of capacities of key conservation actors, in particular agency staff and communities but also other potential partners.

Policy options

6.4.1 Support multi-disciplinary learning and 'learning by doing' of natural resource professionals

Staff of conservation agencies, at both the national and individual protected area level, are crucial actors in fostering (or impeding) the contributions of indigenous and local communities to conservation. Professional training is a good starting point. Much conventional education curricula of natural resource managers deal extensively with biological and environmental subjects but much less so with social and economic matters. A tendency still widespread in some quarters portrays management as an exact science, which needs to be implemented in a top down fashion rather than tested or discussed on the basis of unique and dynamic local contexts. Other training courses, however, have begun to advocate adaptive management as the option of choice and to recognise that new professional capacities are needed to carry this out. The new natural resource managers need inter-disciplinary knowledge, critical analysis and communication skills, and the capacity to deal with the "social face" of conservation.[196] These are best developed through multi-disciplinary learning, and continuing education initiatives based on a "learning by doing" approach. Curricula could include history of natural resource management, anthropology, human rights, pluralism and multiculturalism, gender equity and economic and non-economic valuation of natural resources.[197] As the most significant change likely to confront natural resource professionals is the need to work with society rather than in isolation, the skills to be acquired include participatory methodologies (assessment, research, planning and evaluation), social communication, conflict resolution and mediation. Basic to all of the above is language training, as too often there is little direct dialogue between communities and professionals experts.

The interdisciplinary competence and skills developed in basic education can be deepened though continuing–education initiatives, developed with the active involvement of the relevant professionals and tailored to their needs. In the context of protected

---

[196] Pathak, 2003.

[197] An innovative GEF project in Morocco is currently promoting the entire overhauling of professional training for protected area staff. The new curriculum is being restructured into four broad areas: conservation of biodiversity and landscape/seascapes; sustainable development and the valuing of biodiversity; governance of natural resources and participatory management; and management of protected areas.

areas, support can be given to national and/or international learning networks among Co-managed Protected Areas and Community Conserved Areas, using workshops among relevant actors at different levels, field visits and exchange visits.[198] Policies can also promote field-based workshops for decision-makers, allowing them to be exposed to community-based practices and initiatives and to explore and understand their benefits and the conditions for their existence. This will allow joint (horizontal) learning among peers engaged in participatory management experiences in different regions and countries.

Networks of the kind just mentioned should be assisted, but not directed, by experts. Documented examples and guidelines should be made available to all concerned and to protected area staff in particular. Such flexible processes of learning will allow professionals to develop the skills they need to work in particular situations.[199]

Finally, an important element of professional capacity building is the evaluation of performance. Policy can promote such evaluation exercises and provide financial and career incentives to reward those who build constructive relationships with indigenous and local communities and other social actors.

6.4.2 Assist indigenous and local communities and other social actors to evaluate and address their own capacity for co-management and community conservation

Capacity building for natural resource management and conservation is a demand often made by local communities[200] as well as NGOs and other partners. Supportive policy can begin by promoting participatory assessment exercises (see options 4.2.1 and 5.2.1) and identifying the particular needs (facilitation, legal advice, organising, technical, technological, financial, administrative support, etc.) faced by communities and partners in specific contexts.[201] Although a policy at national level could promote the participatory assessment of capacity building needs in all the protected areas of a country, it is important that no "blanket training" or other forms of support are imposed upon communities but that each decides the capacities it wishes to develop. Members of environmental NGOs, research bodies and academic organizations can also be assisted to evaluate their own capacity needs. Of crucial relevance would be their skills as conveners, supporters of community organizing, facilitators for negotiation and collaborative decision-making processes, and as providers of technical support.

Particular care should be used regarding policy to support the financial capacities of indigenous peoples and local and mobile communities. Conservation demands sizeable investments of time and economic resources (e.g. for demarcation, trail maintenance, inventories, guard stations, monitoring and surveillance, equipment for surveys, communications and information sharing). Since many official protected areas face

---

[198] Nguinguiri, 2000.

[199] Nguinguiri, 2003.

[200] Latin American examples of community-originated capacity building initiatives include those of the Awa people in Ecuador, the Kaa-Iya communities in Bolivia, the Kuna people in Panama, the Zapotec and Chinantec communities in Mexico, and the programmes of the University of the Atlantic Coast in Nicaragua (Oviedo, 2002).

[201] See Chapter 5.

shortages in financial and human resources, it is often very helpful if community members can participate in co-management or take full conservation responsibility in Community Conserved Areas. Yet, community conservation is no exception to economic rules: it, too, involves costs. While such costs may be less than the costs of conservation management by professionals, communities should be helped to raise the financial resources necessary to support their own practices. Policy can address this need by providing, for instance, Community Conservation Funds or assisting in the certification and product labelling systems (such as "certificates of origin", quality control labels, social-equity labels and "good governance" labels). It is also important to put in place policies that evaluate perverse economic incentives, such as tax breaks and subsidies to ecologically destructive industrial plantations, and re-orient them towards incentives for community-based conservation.

6.4.3 Assist in networking at the local, national and international level, in particular among Co-managed Protected Areas, Community Conserved Areas and relevant sources of support

Conservation professionals and communities involved in Co-managed Protected Areas or Community Conserved Areas often feel isolated in their efforts and would greatly profit from exchanges with other protected area sites and initiatives, with other communities and with a variety of social actors working on similar issues. Policy can address these needs by promoting various types of national or regional networks. It can for instance, link field initiatives facing similar problems and opportunities, including both Co-managed Protected Areas and Community Conserved Areas, through regular gatherings, workshops and exchange visits, but also though electronic communication or published newsletters. It is helpful, too, to use field experience to communicate the benefits of community-based approaches to conservation to experts, government agencies, NGOs and international networks dealing with natural resource management. It would be helpful also if countries were to compile and maintain information on such initiatives and on sources of technical and financial support. This might include an updated roster of specialized organizations and individuals, who could be called upon to assist government-managed and Co-managed Protected Areas and Community Conserved Areas.

References

Abrams, P., Borrini-Feyerabend, G., Gardner, J. and Heylings, P. 2003. *Evaluating Governance. A Handbook to Accompany a Participatory Process for a Protected Area.* Report for Parks Canada and CEESP/CMWG/TILCEPA.

Agarwal, A. and Narain, S. 1989. *Towards Green Villages.* Centre for Science and the Environment, New Delhi, India.

Alcorn, J., Luque, A. and Valenzuela, S. 2003. Institutional change: global governance and institutional trends affecting protected areas management. Unpublished background paper prepared for the Ecosystems, People and Parks Project, IUCN World Commission on Protected Areas.

Allali-Puz, H., Bechaux, E. and Jenkins, C. 2003. "Gouvernance et démocratie locale dans les Parcs Naturels Régionaux de France", *Policy Matters* 12: 225–237.

Amend, S. and Amend, T. 1995. *National Parks Without People? The South American Experience.* IUCN, Quito, Ecuador.

Baird, I.G. and Dearden, P. 2003. "Biodiversity conservation and resource tenure regimes: a case study from Northeast Cambodia". *Environmental Management* 32(5): 541–550.

Bajimaja, S.S. 2003. "Nepal's experience in participatory biodiversity conservation with emphasis on buffer zone initiatives". *Policy Matters* 12: 276–282.

Baldus, R., Kibunde, B. and Siege, L. 2003. "Seeking conservation partnerships in the Selous Game Reserve, Tanzania". *Parks* 13(1): 50–61.

Banuri, T. and Najam, A. 2002. *Civic Entrepreneurship: A Civil Society Perspective on Sustainable Development.* SEI, UNEP and RING for Gandhara Academy Press, Islamabad, Pakistan.

Barton, T., Borrini-Feyerabend, G., de Sherbinin, A. and Warren, P. 1997. *Our People, Our Resources. Supporting Rural Communities in Participatory Action Research on Population Dynamics and the Local Environment.* IUCN, Gland, Switzerland and Cambridge, UK. Available also in French and Spanish. www.iucn.org/themes/spg/opor/opor.html.

Bassi, M. 2003. "Enhancing equity in the relationship between protected areas and local communities in the context of global change: horn of Africa and Kenya". TILCEPA report. www.iucn.org/themes/ceesp/Wkg_grp/TILCEPA/community.htm#A.

Beltrán, J. (Ed.) 2000. *Indigenous and Traditional Peoples and Protected Areas: Principles, Guidelines and Case Studies.* IUCN, Gland, Switzerland and Cambridge, UK and WWF International, Gland, Switzerland.

Bennett, A.F. 1998. *Linkages in the Landscape: The Role of Corridors and Connectivity in Wildlife Conservation.* IUCN, Gland, Switzerland and Cambridge, UK.

Beresford, M. and Phillips, A. 2000. "Protected landscapes: a conservation model for the 21st Century". *The George Wright Forum* 17:1.

Berkes, F., George, P. and Preston, R.J. 1991. "Co-management". *Alternatives* 18(2): 12–18.

Bishop, K., Dudley, N., Phillips, A. and Stolton, S. [in press]. *Speaking a Common Language.* Cardiff University and IUCN, Gland, Switzerland and Cambridge, UK.

Bormann, F.H. and Likens, G.E. 1979. *Pattern and Process in a Forested Ecosystem.* Springer Verlag, New York, USA.

Borrini, G. 1992. *Environment and "Health as a Sustainable State". Concepts, Terms and Resources for a Primary Health Care Manager in Developing Countries.* ICHM, Istituto Superiore di Sanità, Rome, Italy.

Borrini-Feyerabend, G. 1996. *Collaborative Management of Protected Areas: Tailoring the Approach to the Context.* IUCN, Gland, Switzerland. www.iucn.org/themes/spg/Files/ tailor.html.

Borrini-Feyerabend, G. (Ed.) 1997. (reprinted 2001). *Beyond Fences: Seeking Social Sustainability in Conservation.* 2 vols. IUCN, Gland, Switzerland and Cambridge, UK. www.iucn.org/themes/spg/Files/beyond_fences/beyond_fences.html.

Borrini-Feyerabend, G. 2003. "Governance of protected areas: innovations in the air … ". *Policy Matters* 12: 92–101.

Borrini-Feyerabend, G. 2004. "Governance of protected areas, participation and equity" in Secretariat of the Convention on Biological Diversity (SCBD), *Biodiversity Issues for Consideration in the Planning, Establishment and Management of Protected Area Sites and Networks.* SCBD, Montreal, Canada.

Borrini-Feyerabend, G. and Sandwith, T. 2003. "From guns and fences to paternalism to partner-ships: the slow disentangling of Africa's protected areas" *Parks* 13(1): 1–5. www.iucn.org/ themes/ceesp/Publications/TILCEPA/Editorial–13_1.pdf.

Borrini-Feyerabend, G., Pimbert, M., Farvar, M.T., Kothari, A. and Renard, Y. 2004 [in press]. *Sharing Power – Learning by Doing in Co-management of Natural Resources throughout the World.* IIED and IUCN/CEESP/CMWG (Ed.) Cenesta, Teheran, Iran.

Boyd, C. 2004. "Protected landscapes, corridors, connectivity and ecological networks" in Secretariat of the Convention on Biological Diversity (SCBD), *Biodiversity Issues for Consideration in the Planning, Establishment and Management of Protected Area Sites and Networks.* SCBD, Montreal, Canada.

Brechin, S.R., Wilshusen, P.R., Fortwangler, C.L. and West, P. 2003. *Contested Nature – Promoting International Biodiversity with Social Justice in the Twenty-first Century.* State University of New York Press, Albany, USA.

Brockington, D. 2003. "Injustice and conservation: is 'local support' necessary for sustainable conservation?" *Policy Matters* 12: 22–30.

CBD Secretariat. 2003. *Handbook of the Convention on Biological Diversity,* CBD, UN and UNEP, Montreal, Canada.

CBD. Programme of Work on Protected Areas, approved at COP 7, Kuala Lumpur, February 2004. www.biodiv.org/decisions/default.aspx?m=COP–07&id=7765&lg=0.

Cernea, M. and Schmidt-Soltau, K. 2003. "The end of forcible displacements? conservation must not impoverish people". *Policy Matters* 12: 42–51.

Cernea, M.M. (Ed.) 1985. *Putting People First.* Oxford University Press, New York, USA.

Chape, S., Blyth, S., Fish, L., Fox, P. and Spalding, M. 2003. *2003 United Nations List of Protected Areas.* IUCN, Gland, Switzerland and Cambridge, UK and UNEP World Conserva-tion Monitoring Centre, Cambridge, UK.

Colchester, M. 2003. *Salvaging Nature – Indigenous Peoples, Protected Areas and Biodiversity Conservation.* World Rainforest Movement and Forests Peoples Programme, Moreton in Marsh, UK.

Davey, A. 1998. *National System Planning for Protected Areas.* IUCN, Gland, Switzerland and Cambridge, UK.

Eghenter, C. and Labo, M. 2003. "In search of equitable governance models for indigenous peoples in protected areas – the experience of Kayan Mentarang National Park". *Policy Matters* 12: 248–253.

FENAMAD (Federacion Nativa del Rio Madre de Dios y Afluentes). 2002. "Se Crea Reserva Comunal Amarakaeri: Logro Del Pueblo Harakmbut, De Fenamad Y Del Movimiento Popular De Madre De Dios". Puerto Maldonado (Peru), press release, 13 May.

Ferrari, M.F. 2002. *Synthesis of Lessons Learned in the Establishment and Management of Protected Areas by Indigenous and Local Communities in South-East Asia*. Report for TILCEPA. www.iucn.org/themes/ceesp/Publications/TILCEPA/CCA-MFerrari-part1.pdf and www.iucn.org/themes/ceesp/Publications/TILCEPA/CCA-MFerrari-part2.pdf.

Ferrari, M.F. and de Vera, D. 2003. "A "participatory"or a "rights-based"approach? Which is best for protected areas and indigenous peoples in the Philippines?" *Policy Matters* 12: 166–170.

Fiedler, P.L. and Jain, S.K. (Eds.) 1992. *Conservation Biology: The Theory and Practice of Nature Conservation, Preservation and Management*. Routledge, London, UK.

Forman, R.T.T. and Godron, M. 1986. *Landscape Ecology*. John Wiley and Sons, New York, USA.

Ghai, D. and Vivian, J.M. 1992. *Grassroots Environmental Action*. Routledge, London, UK and New York, USA.

Ghimire, K.B. and Pimbert, M.P. (Eds.) 1997. *Social Change and Conservation – Environmental Politics and Impacts of National Parks and Protected Areas*. UNRISD and Earthscan, London, UK.

Gladu, J.P., Brubacher, D. and Meek, C. 2003. "Aboriginal experiences in Canada – parks and protected areas". Boreal Footprint Project, Taiga Rescue Network.

Gonzalez, T. and Arce, J. 2001. *Los pueblos indígenas y la conservación de la diversidad biológica en América Latina*. Paper presented in Puerto Maldonado, Perú, 17–19 October, 2001.

Graham, J., Amos, B. and Plumptre, T. 2003. "Governance principles for protected areas in the 21st century". A discussion paper, phase 2, in collaboration with Parks Canada and Canadian International Development Agency, Canada.

Gunderson, L. and Holling, C. (Eds.) 2002. *Panarchy*. Island Press, Washington DC, USA.

Gunderson, L.H. and Pritchard, L.J. 2002. *Resilience and the Behavior of Large Scale Systems*. Island Press, Washington DC, USA.

Harmon, D. 1991. "National park residency in developed countries: the example of Great Britain". In West and Brechin (1991).

Harmon, D. 2003. "Intangible values of protected areas". *Policy Matters* 12: 55–63.

Hayes, S. and Shultis, J. 2001. *Implementation of an Exchange Programme for Protected Areas in East Asia*. IUCN, Gland, Switzerland and Cambridge, UK.

Heylings, P. and Bravo, M. 2001. "Survival of the fittest? challenges facing the co-management model for the Galapagos Marine Reserve". *CM News* 5: 10–13.

Hockings, M., Stolton, S. and Dudley, N. 2000. *Evaluating Effectiveness – A Framework for Assessing the Management of Protected Areas*. Best Practice Protected Area Guidelines Series. IUCN, Gland, Switzerland and Cambridge, UK.

Holling, C.S. (Ed.) 1978. *Adaptive Environmental Assessment and Management*. John Wiley and Sons, London, UK.

ICSU (International Council for Science). 2002. *Resilience and Sustainable Development: Building Adaptive Capacity in a World of Transformations*. ICSU Series on Science for Sustainable Development n.3, Paris, France.

IUCN. 1994.*Guide to the Convention on Biological Diversity*. IUCN, Gland, Switzerland and Cambridge, UK.

IUCN. 1996. *World Conservation*, special issue on collaborative management, No.2.

IUCN. 1998. "IUCN gender policy statement", available on the web: www.iucn.org/themes/spg/Files/gender_policy.pdf, adopted by IUCN Council in April 2000.

IUCN. 2000. "Policy on social equity in conservation and sustainable use of natural resources", available on the web: www.iucn.org/themes/spg/Files/equity_policy.pdf, adopted by IUCN Council, February 2000.

IUCN/CEESP. 2002. *Policy Matters* 10, special issue on Co-management of Natural Resources and Sustainable Livelihoods. www.iucn.org/themes/ceesp/Publications/newsletter/Policy%20Matters%2010.pdf

IUCN/CEESP. 2003. *Policy Matters* 12, special issue on Community Empowerment for Conservation. Www.iucn.org/themes/ceesp/Publications/newsletter/PM12.pdf

IUCN, CNPPA and WCMC. 1994. *Guidelines for Protected Area Management Categories.* IUCN, Gland, Switzerland and Cambridge, UK.

IUCN, UNEP and WWF. 1991. *Caring for the Earth*. IUCN, Gland, Switzerland and Cambridge, UK.

Jaireth, H. and Smyth, D. (Eds.) 2003. *Innovative Governance: Indigenous Peoples, Local Communities, and Protected Areas.* Ane Books, New Delhi, India.

Jeanrenaud, S. 2001. "Communities and forest management in Western Europe", a regional profile of the working group on community involvement in forest management. *People, Forests and Policies*. IUCN, Gland, Switzerland.

Jones, B. 2003. "Enhancing equity in the relationship between protected areas and indigenous and local communities in the context of global change: lessons learned from the philosophy and practice of CBNRM in Southern Africa". www.iucn.org/themes/ceesp/Publications/TILCEPA/CCA-BJones.pdf

Kothari, A., Singh, N. and Suri, S. (Eds.) 1996. *People and Protected Areas: towards Participatory Conservation in India.* Sage Publications, New Delhi, India.

Kothari, A., Anuradha, R.V., Pathak, N. and Taneja, B. (Eds.) 1998. *Communities and Conservation*. Sage, New Delhi, India and London, UK.

Kothari, A., Vania, F., Das, P., Christopher, K. and Jha, S. 1997. *Building Bridges for Conservation*. Indian Institute of Public Administration, New Delhi, India.

Kothari, A., Pathak, N. and Vania, F. 2000. *Where Communities Care: Community Based Wildlife and Ecosystem Management in South Asia*. International Institute of Environment and Development, London, UK and Kalpavriksh, Pune, India.

Kothari, A. (with others). 2003. "Community conserved areas and the international conservation system – a discussion note relating to the mandate of the WCPA/CEESP Theme Group on Indigenous/Local Communities, Equity, and Protected Areas(TILCEPA)". Manuscript, available on: www.iucn.org/themes/ceesp/Wkg_grp/TILCEPA/TILCEPA.htm#cca.

Laird, S.A. (Ed.) 2002. *Biodiversity and Traditional Knowledge: Equitable Partnerships in Practice*. Earthscan, London, UK.

Larsen, P.B. 2000. "Co-managing protected areas with indigenous peoples: a global overview for IUCN/WCPA and WWF". WWF International, manuscript.

Larsen, P.B. 2003. "IUCN social policy related to protected areas: a thematic analysis". IUCN Social Policy Programme, manuscript.

Lucas, P.H.C. 1992. *Protected Landscapes for Policy Makers and Planners*. Chapman and Hall, London, UK.

Luckett, S., Khulani, M. and Potter, D. 2003. "The experience of local boards in KwaZulu Natal, South Africa". *Parks* 13(1): 6–15.

Luken, J.O. 1990. *Directing Ecological Succession*, Chapman and Hall, New York.

Luque, A. 2003. "The people of the Matavén Forest and the national park system – allies in the creation of a Community Conserved Area in Colombia". *Policy Matters* 12: 145–151.

MacDonald, K.I. 2003. *Community-Based Conservation: A Reflection on History*. Report for TILCEPA. www.iucn.org/themes/ceesp/Publications/TILCEPA/CCA-KMacDonald.pdf.

MacKay, F. 2002. *Addressing Past Wrongs. Indigenous Peoples and Protected Areas: The Right to Restitution of Lands and Resources*. Forest Peoples Programme. http://forestpeoples.gn.apc.org/Briefings/Indigenous%20Rights/ips_restitution_protected_areas_oct02_eng.htm.

Maldidier, C. 2000. La décentralisation de la gestion des ressources renouvelables à Madagascar – Les premiers enseignements sur les processus en cours et les méthodes d'intervention. Manuscript, Office National de l'Environnement, Madagascar.

McNeely, J.A. (Ed.) 1995. *Expanding Partnerships in Conservation*. Island Press, Washington DC, USA.

MEA (Millennium Ecosystem Assessment). 2003. *Ecosystems and Human Well-being*. Island Press, Washington DC, USA.

Merlo, M., Morandini, R., Gabbrielli, A. and Novaco, I. 1989. *Collective Forest Land Tenure and Rural Development in Italy: Selected Case Studies*. FO: MISC/()/10, FAO, Rome, Italy.

MoEF and Kalpavriksh. [in press]. *National Biodiversity Strategy and Action Plan: Final Technical Report of the UNDP-GEF Sponsored Project*. Ministry of Environment and Forests, Government of India and Kalpavriksh, Delhi/Pune, India.

Molnar, A., Scherr, S. and Khare, A. 2003. "Who conserves the world's forests: community driven strategies to protect forests and respect rights". Paper presented in the Conservation Finance Stream, World Parks Congress, Durban, South Africa.

Momberg, F., Atok, K. and Siriat, M. 1996. *Drawing on Local Knowledge: A Community Mapping Training Manual*. World Wide Fund for Nature, Yayasan Karya Sosial Pancur Kasih and Ford Foundation, Jakarta, Indonesia.

Mulongoy, K.J. and Chape, S. 2004. *Protected Areas and Biodiversity: An Overview of Key Issues*. CBD Secretariat, Montreal, Canada and UNEP-WCMC, Cambridge, UK.

Nguinguiri, J.C. 2000. "Collective learning on collaborative management of natural resources in the Congo Basin: the First Lessons". *CM News* 4: 2–3.

Nguinguiri, J.C. 2003. "Gouvernance des aires protégées: l'importance des 'normes pratiques' de régulation de la gestion locale pour la faisabilité des réformes dans le Bassin du Congo". *Policy Matters* 12: 16–21.

NRTEE. 1998. *Sustainable Strategies for Oceans: a Co-management Guide*. National Round Table on the Environment and the Economy (NRTEE), Ottawa, Canada.

Okello, M., Seno, S.O. and Wishitemi, B. 2003. "Maasai community wildlife sanctuaries in Tsavo-Amboseli, Kenya". *Parks* 13(1): 62–74.

Otegui, M. 2003. "Wirikuta, the Huichol Sacred Space in the Chihuahuan Desert of San Luis Potosí, Mexico". Report presented at the IUCN V[th] World Congress on Protected Areas, Stream on Building Support for Protected Areas. Durban, South Africa.

Oviedo, G. 2002. "Lessons learned in the establishment and management of protected areas by indigenous and local communities, South America: enhancing equity in the relationship between protected areas and indigenous and local communities in the context of global change". www.iucn.org/themes/ceesp/Publications/TILCEPA/CCA-GOviedo.pdf

Oviedo, G. 2003a. "Some notes on PA definitions and categories, with special reference to reforming the PA system to accommodate the interests of indigenous peoples and local communities". IUCN Social Policy Programme, manuscript.

Oviedo, G. 2003b. "Indigenous peoples issues in the IUCN". IUCN Internal Discussion Note, Draft 21, www.iucn.org.

Oviedo, G., Maffi, L. and Larsen, P.B. 2000. "Indigenous and traditional peoples of the world and ecoregion conservation, an integrated approach to conserving the world's biological and cultural diversity". WWF International and Terralingua.

Pathak, N. 2003. "Lessons learnt in the establishment and management of protected areas by indigenous and local communities in South Asia". TILCEPA report. www.iucn.org/themes/ceesp/Wkg_grp/TILCEPA/community.htm#A.

Pathak, N. and Bhushan, S. 2004. "Community Reserves". *Survey of the Environment.* The Hindu, Chennai, India.

Pathak, N., Choudhury, S. and Bandekar, R. 2004. Community Conserved Areas in India: analysis and case studies. Kalpavriksh, Pune, India. Draft manuscript.

Phillips, A. 2002. *Management Guidelines for IUCN Category V Protected Areas: Protected Landscapes/Seascapes.* Best Practice Protected Area Guidelines Series. IUCN, Gland, Switzerland and Cambridge, UK.

Phillips, A. 2003. "Turning ideas on their head: the new paradigm for protected areas". *The George Wright Forum* 20(2).

Pickett, S. and Thompson, J.N. 1978. "Patch dynamics and the design of nature reserves". *Biological Conservation* 13: 27–37.

Plant, R. and Hvalkof, S. 2001. *Land Titling and Indigenous Peoples,* Technical Papers Series, Inter-American Development Bank, Sustainable Development Department, Washington DC, USA.

Polanyi, K. 1957. *The Great Transformation.* Beacon Press, Boston, USA.

Poole, P. 1995. *Indigenous Peoples, Mapping & Biodiversity Conservation, and Analysis of Current Activities and Opportunities for Applying Geomatics Technologies.* Peoples and Forest Program Discussion Paper, Biodiversity Support Program (BSP), Washington, DC, USA.

Posey, D.A. 1998. "Introduction: culture and nature – the inextricable link". In Posey, D.A. (Ed.) *Cultural and Spiritual Values of Biodiversity.* Intermediate Technology Publications, London, UK.

Pye-Smith, C. and Borrini-Feyerabend, G. 1994. *The Wealth of Communities.* Earthscan, London, UK.

Ralston, L., Anderson, J. and Colson, E. 1983. *Voluntary Efforts in Decentralized Management.* Institute of International Studies, University of California, Research Series no. 53, Berkeley, USA.

Ramsar Convention Secretariat. 2004. *Ramsar Handbooks for the Wise Use of Wetlands.* 2nd edition. Ramsar Convention Secretariat, Gland, Switzerland.

Reader, J. 1990. *Man on Earth.* Penguin Books, London, UK.

Renard, Y. 1997. "Collaborative management for conservation". In Borrini-Feyerabend (1997).

Ribot, J.C. 2002. *Democratic Decentralisation of Natural Resources.* WRI, Washington DC, USA.

Roldán Ortega, R. 2002. Derechos de los Pueblos y Comunidades Indígenas a la Tierra. Aspectos Legales e Institucionales. Banco Mundial, Taller Regional sobre Políticas de Tierras. Pachuca, México, Mayo 19–22, 2002.

Sandwith, T., Shine, C., Hamilton, L. and Sheppard, D. 2001. *Transboundary Protected Areas for Peace and Co-operation.* IUCN, Gland, Switzerland and Cambridge, UK.

Saragoussi, M., Pinheiro, M., Chavez, M., Murchie, A. and Borges, S. 2002. "An experiment in participatory mapping in Brasil's Jau National Park". In Wood, C.H. and Porro, R. (Eds.) *Deforestation and Land Use in the Amazon*. Florida University Press, Gainesville, USA.

Shresth, S. with Devidas, S. 2001. *Forest Revival and Traditional Water Harvesting: Community Based Conservation at Bhaonta-Kolyala, Rajasthan, India*. Kalpavriksh, Pune, India and IIED, London, UK.

Smyth, D. 2001. "Joint management of national parks in Australia". In Baker, R., Davies, J. and Young, E. (Eds.) *Working on Country – Contemporary Indigenous Management of Australia's Lands and Coastal Regions*. Oxford University Press, Oxford, UK.

Solis Rivera, V., Madrigal Cordero, P., Ayales Cruz, I., y Fonseca Borras, M. 2003. *Equidad entre Áreas Protegidas y Comunidades Locales: Reflexion desde Mesoamérica y el Caribe*. CoopeSolidar, R.L., San José, Costa Rica.

Stanciu, E. 2001. "First steps towards collaborative management of Retezat National Park, Romania". *CM News* 6: 7.

Statham, D.K. 1994. "The farm scheme of North York Moors National Park, United Kingdom". In Western and Wright (1994).

Steenkamp, C. 2002. "Balancing the powers in Makuleke land". *Policy Matters* 10: 77–79.

Steins, N.A. and Edwards, V.M. 1999. "Platforms for collective action in multiple-use common-pool resources". *Agriculture and Human Values* 16: 241–255.

Stevens, S. (Ed.) 1997. *Conservation through Cultural Survival*. Island Press, Washington DC, USA.

Stolton, S. and Dudley, N. (Eds.) 1999. *Partnerships for Protection: New Strategies for Planning and Management of Protected Areas*. Earthscan, London, UK.

Thomas, L. and Middleton, J. 2003. *Guidelines for Management Planning of Protected Areas*. IUCN, Gland, Switzerland and Cambridge, UK.

Turner, M.G., Gardner, R.H. and O'Neill, R.V. 2001. *Landscape Ecology in Theory and Practice*. Springer Verlag, New York, USA.

UN Millennium Development Goals. www.un.org/millenniumgoals/.

UNDP (United Nations Development Programme). 1999. *Human Development Report 1999: Globalisation with a Human Face*. UNDP, New York, USA.

UNDP. 2002. *Human Development Report 2002: Deepening Democracy in a Fragmented World*. UNDP, New York, USA.

UNESCO. 1995. "The Seville strategy for biosphere reserves". *Nature and Resources* 31(2): 2–10.

Walters, C.J. 1986. *Adaptive Management of Renewable Resources*. McGraw-Hill, New York, USA.

West, P.C. and Brechin, S.R. (Eds.) 1991. *Resident Peoples and National Parks*. University of Arizona Press, Tucson, USA.

Western, D. and Wright, R.M. 1994. *Natural Connections*. Island Press, Washington DC, USA.

White, A.T., Zeitlin Hale, L., Renard, Y. and Cortesi, L. 1994. *Collaborative and Community-based Management of Coral Reefs: Lessons from Experience*. Kumarian Press, West Hartford, USA.

Whittaker, R.H. and Levin, S.A. 1977. "The role of mosaic phenomena in natural communities". *Theory of Population Biology* 12: 117–139.

Wilson, A. 2003. "All parks are people's parks". *Policy Matters* 12: 71–75.

Winer, N. 2001. "Co-management in Southern Bolivia: a form of territorial recognition for the

Guarani Izoceno People". *CM News* 5: 21–22.

Winer, N. 2003. "Co-management of protected areas, the oil and gas industry and indigenous empowerment – the experience of Bolivia's Kaa Iya del Gran Chaco". *Policy Matters* 12: 181–191.

Worah, S. 2002. "The challenge of community-based protected area management". *Parks* 12(2): 80–90.

WWF. 2002. "Community protected natural areas in the state of Oaxaca, Mexico". WWF Forests for Life and WWF Mexico Programme.

WRI. 2003. *World Resources 2002–2004 – Decisions for the Earth: Balance, Voice and Power.* UNDP, UNEP, WB, WRI, Washington DC, USA.

Zuluaga, G., Giraldo, J.I. and Jiménez Larrarte, M. 2003. "Un ejemplo de conservacion bio-cultural: el Parque Nacional Natural Alto Fragua-Indiwasi en Colombia". *Policy Matters* 12: 171–180.

Suggested additional reading

Aguilar, L., Castañeda, I. and Salazar, H. 2002. *In Search of the Lost Gender: Equity in Protected Areas.* IUCN, WCPA, Social Programme, Mesoamerican Office, Asoluto SA.

Ali, I. and Butz, D. 2003. "The Shimshal governance model – a Community Conserved Area, a sense of cultural identity, a way of life … ". *Policy Matters* 12: 111–120.

Amadou, B., Vogt, G. and Vogt, K. 2003. "Developing a community conserved area in Niger". *Parks* 13(1): 16–27.

Anon. 2004. Workshop on Community Reserves, Conservation Reserves, and Other Legal Spaces for Community Conserved Areas, 3–4 February 2004, Summary of Discussions and Recommendations. www.kalpavriksh.org.

Bah, H., Boubout, A. and Boujou, S. 2003. "Micro-finance et conservation dans le Parc National du Diawling". *Policy Matters* 12: 270–275.

Borrini-Feyerabend, G., Farvar, M.T., Nguinguiri, J.C. and Ndangang, V.A. 2000. *Co-management of Natural Resources: Organising, Negotiating and Learning-by-Doing.* GTZ and IUCN, Kasparek Verlag, Heidelberg, Germany. http://nrm.massey.ac.nz/changelinks/cmnr.html.

Botkin, D.B. and Sobel, M.J. 1975. "Stability in time-varying ecosystems". *American Naturalist* 109: 65–46.

Bromley, D.W. and Cernea, M. 1989. The management of common property natural resources: some conceptual fallacies, *World Bank Discussion Paper* 57. Washington DC, USA.

Chhetri, P., Mugisha, A. and White, S. 2003. "Community resource use in Kibale and Mt. Elgon National Parks, Uganda". *Parks* 13(1): 28–38.

Dubos, R. 1980. *Man Adapting.* Yale University Press, New Haven, USA and London, UK.

IUCN/BRAO. 2003. Atelier sur la gouvernance des aires protégées d'Afrique: Rapport de synthèse – Atelier tenu à la Kompienga (Burkina Faso), 25–28 mars 2003. UICN-CIRAD-Ministère français des affaires étrangères. Ouagadougou, Burkina Faso.

IUCN, MAE (France) et CIRAD. 2003. What Governance for Protected Areas in Subsaharian Africa?, Report of the Kompienga Workshop. Ouagadougou, Burkina Faso.

Iwan, R. 2003. "Setulang village protects its river!" *Policy Matters* 12: 152–153.

Jones, B.T.B. and Chonguica, E. 2001. "Review and Analysis of Specific Trans Boundary Natural Resource Management (TBNRM) initiatives in the southern African Region". IUCN-ROSA, Harare, Zimbabwe.

Kamstra, J. 1994. *Protected Areas: towards a Participatory Approach.* Netherlands Committee for IUCN, Amsterdam, Netherlands.

Lewis, C. (Ed.) 1996. *Managing Conflicts in Protected Areas.* IUCN, Gland, Switzerland.

Long, F.J. and Arnold, M.B. 1995. *The Power of Environmental Partnerships.* The Dryden Press, Fort Worth, USA.

McNaughton, S.J. 1989. "Ecosystems and conservation in the twenty-first century". In Western, D. and Pearl, M.C. (Eds.) *Conservation for the Twenty-first Century.* Oxford University Press, New York, USA.

McNeely, J.A. (Ed.) 1993. *Parks for Life: Report of the IVth World Congress on National Parks and Protected Areas.* IUCN/WCPA, Gland, Switzerland.

Murphree, M.W. 1991. *Communities as Institutions for Resource Management*. Center for Applied Social Sciences (CASS), University of Zimbabwe, Harare, Zimbabwe.

Pimbert, M. and Wakeford, T. (Eds.) 2001. Deliberative democracy and citizen empowerment, Special Issue of *PLA Notes* 40. IIED, London, UK.

Taty, M., Chatelain, C. and Borrini-Feyerabend, G. 2003. "An impressive yet vulnerable co-management partnership in Congo". *Parks* 13(1): 39–49.

Taylor, B. An Introductory Guide to Adaptive Management. Ministry of Forests, Canada. www.for.gov.bc.ca/hfp/amhome/introgd/toc.htm.

Thiaw, W., Sylla, S.I. and Larivière, J. 2003. "Les Aires du Patrimoine Communautaire – les paradoxes de la conservation au Sénégal". *Policy Matters* 12: 156–165.